325
Tow.

88382

Townsend, Peter
The Girl in the White
Ship

DATE DUE			

The Girl in the White Ship

By the same author

Earth My Friend
Duel of Eagles
The Last Emperor
Time and Chance: An Autobiography
The Smallest Pawns in the Game

Peter Townsend

The Girl
in the
White Ship

HOLT, RINEHART and WINSTON
New York

First published in the United States in 1983 by
Holt, Rinehart and Winston, 383 Madison Avenue,
New York, New York 10017.

Library of Congress Cataloging in Publication Data
Townsend, Peter, 1914–
The girl in the white ship.
1. Refugees, Political—Vietnam.   2. Chinese—
Vietnam.   3. Vietnam—Politics and government—
1975–   . I. Title.
DS559.912.T68 1983   325′.21′09597   82-3110
ISBN: 0-03-057787-X   AACR2

First American Edition

Design: Ellen LoGiudice
Printed in the United States of America
1   3   5   7   9   10   8   6   4   2

ISBN 0-03-057787-X

In memory of Tran Dieu Trung

ACKNOWLEDGMENTS

In order to write the story of Tran Hue Hue I had to seek much help and information, apart from that so readily given by Hue Hue and her family, from many other people and organizations. For their willing and friendly cooperation, I am deeply grateful to:

In Geneva
The office of the United Nations High Commissioner for Refugees, and in particular John Woodward, Nicole Spuhler, Philippe Labreveaux, and Norma Fraser.

In Philippines
Manfred Paeffgen, UNHCR representative, Manila;
Commodore Gil Fernandez, commander in chief, WESCOM, Puerto Princesa, Palawan;
Colonel Igualdad Cunanan, Philippines Constabulary;
Colonel Javelosa, Philippines Air Force, WESCOM, and his helicopter crew;
Colonel Hugo Javier, chief medical officer, WESCOM;
Captain Mariano Tuvilla, Philippines Navy, WESCOM;

Commander Bong Bungag, commanding, Naval Base, Balabac;

Lieutenant Commander Alberto Banzon, Philippines Navy, WESCOM;

Lieutenant Colonel Rodolfo Biazon, commanding, 2nd Marine Brigade, Samariñana;

Commander Ben Doria, Philippines Navy, commanding the frigate LF 50, *La Union*;

Chief Petty Officer Perez, commanding the patrol vessel PCF 319;

Lieutenant Martin Pagaduan, commandant, U5 Refugee Camp, Palawan;

Le Vinh Qui, Chairman, U5 Refugee Camp;

Hadji Hussein, Barangay Chairman (mayor), Mangsee Reef;

Mucktal Hadji Kamaruddin, "patron" of motor vessel *Sittirazma*; his brothers, Hadji Nasser, Motong, and Kadrie, and members of the crew.

My debt to Commodore Fernandez is a very special one. His help and that of the officers and men of his command was indispensable and generously given. Señora Edna, public relations attachée at the Rafols Hotel, Puerto Princesa, greatly assisted my liaison with HQ WESCOM.

In Malaysia
Ali Mohammed, UNHCR Representative, Kuala Lumpur;

Rajiv Kapur, UNHCR, Kuala Lumpur;

Fabrigio Gentilloni, UNHCR, Kuala Trengganu; Uwe, his assistant, who accompanied me to Pulau Bidong;

the Malaysian Police, Trengganu and Pulau Bidong;

Datin Ruby Lee, Secretary General, Malaysian Red Crescent Society;

Mrs. E. S. Naidu, Assistant Secretary, Tracing and Mail Service, MRCS.

In Australia
Veronica Bull, Assistant UNHCR, Sydney;
Department of Immigration and Ethnic Affairs, Australian Government, and especially: Liz Davis, Migrant Service Section, Mrs. Nga ("Angie"), and Mrs. Hienh, interpreters;
George Marley, director, Government Hostel, East Hills;
Mrs. Val Lillas, who provided a temporary home for Hue Hue;
Ly To, Hue Hue's guardian until her parents arrived.

In England
Mrs. S. F. Fellows, librarian, *The Economist*, London;
Mr. T. M. Dinan, librarian, Lloyds, London;
Brian Court-Mappin, member of Lloyds;
Lieutenant A. C. F. David, Hydrographic Department of the Admiralty;
Paul Ridgeway, Trinity House Lighthouse Service;
Mr. J. A. Jackson, Senior Manager, The Salvage Association, London;
Dr. P. T. van de Merwe, Historical Section, National Maritime Museum;
Lieutenant Commander Charles Stuart, RN, for his researches at the National Maritime Museum;
Michael Burton, Maritime, Aviation and Environment Department, Foreign and Commonwealth Office.
The photograph of the white ship is by courtesy of the Salvage Association.

Of great help in providing background information were three excellent publications: *The Boat People*, an *Age* (Melbourne) investigation, edited by Bruce Grant (Penguin Books, 1979); *Boat People*, edited by Ando Isamu, S.J. (Tokyo: Asian Relations Center, Sophia University, 1978); *Le Goulag Vietnamien*, by Doan Van Toai (Paris: Robert Laffont/Opera Mundi, 1979).

In France
Duong Chi Hoa and her husband, Châm, and Ly Van Trung, for their help in matters Vietnamese;
Julia Durand Barquez, Valerie Wunderlich, and Dana Noyé for their valiant efforts in typing the tape transcriptions and the manuscript.

The Girl in the White Ship

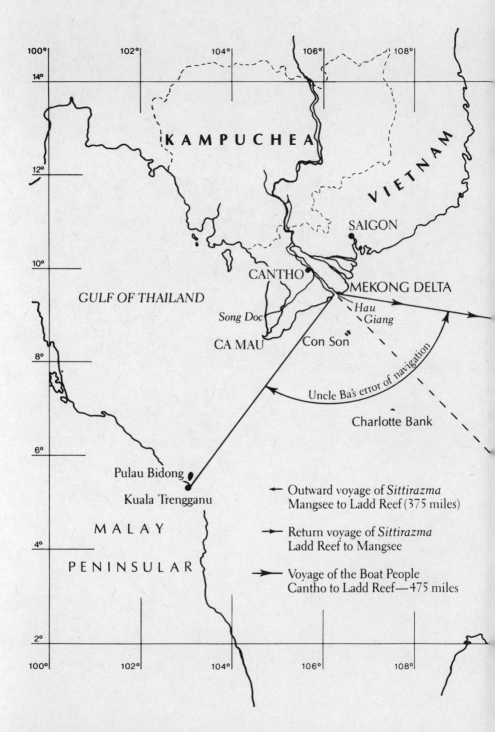

100°   102°   104°   106°   108°

14°

K A M P U C H E A

12°

V I E T N A M

SAIGON

10°

CANTHO   MEKONG DELTA

GULF OF THAILAND

Hau
Giang

Song Doc

8°

CA MAU   Con Son

Uncle Ba's error of navigation

Charlotte Bank

6°

Pulau Bidong

Kuala Trengganu

M A L A Y

4°

P E N I N S U L A R

2°

100°   102°   104°   106°   108°

← Outward voyage of *Sittirazma*
Mangsee to Ladd Reef (375 miles)

→ Return voyage of *Sittirazma*
Ladd Reef to Mangsee

→ Voyage of the Boat People
Cantho to Ladd Reef—475 miles

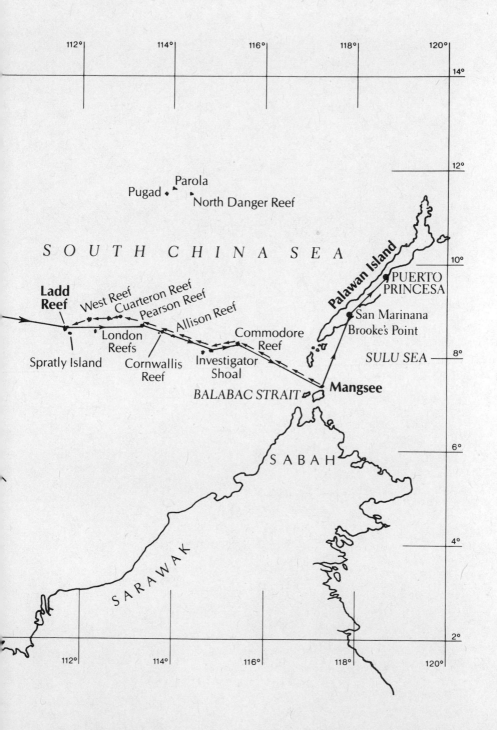

FOREWORD

The "boat people," at least half of whom were young children and teenagers when they fled Vietnam, are but a fraction of the world's refugee population, at present estimated at some fifteen million. As with all refugees, whole families were forced to leave their country because of political, racial, or religious persecution. But the boat people are different in that the sea provided their only way of escape—an extremely hazardous one-way journey with no fixed destination and one that, for hundreds of thousands of them, ended on the ocean bed.

With the defeat of South Vietnam by the Communist North in April 1975, followed by the new government's restrictions on individual freedom, the Vietnamese began to flee their country by boat.

By mid-1979, the boat people numbered nearly 300,000—survivors, that is; almost as many had been lost at sea. Of the survivors, about one third had been resettled in a score of countries as far-flung as Sweden and New Zealand, Paraguay and Luxembourg. The remaining two thirds still lingered on in refugee camps in the Far East.

It was then that delegates from sixty-five countries, including Vietnam and its ally the Soviet Union, met in Geneva to seek a solution to the tragedy. Vietnam made promises, the United Nations took measures; the situation improved; but the boat people, despite the dangers, kept on coming.

There was in Vietnam a large community of ethnic Chinese whose ancestors, driven by social strife and natural disasters such as flood and famine, had immigrated mainly during the seventeenth and nineteenth centuries. In 1978 they numbered some 1.7 million, all but about a quarter of a million of whom lived in the South. Hardworking and astute, they prospered in a number of trades; in rice, Vietnam's main export, they established a monopoly.

Vietnam's great neighbor China is a traditional enemy. After its victory over the South, North Vietnam, though Communist too, regarded its ethnic Chinese citizens not only as undesirable capitalists but as a possible fifth column in the event of war with China. The Vietnamese government's harsh economic measures in 1978 put thousands of ethnic Chinese out of business; thousands more were fired from their posts in the administration. Chinese in jobs like fishing and farming were not spared either. Those living in the North fled by thousands across the frontier into China, or by boat to Hong Kong. In the South many more thousands took to the sea. The flight of the boat people then became a disorderly, massive exodus.

I first became involved with the boat people in 1978 when working on a previous book. I talked to them, children and grown-ups, in their crowded hostels in Singapore, Kuala Lumpur, Hong Kong, Tokyo, and London, in their bamboo huts by the seashore at Laemsing, Thailand, and at Pulau Bidong, the island camp off the Malaysian coast.

I was moved to write this book after listening to the stories of

2

some of these recklessly brave but mostly inexperienced seafarers. There was Lan, the fisherman, a Catholic, who left Communist Vietnam in his own boat in search of a country where his ten children could receive a Christian education; seven of the children—and the boat—were lost at sea. Then there were Trang and Vu, angel-faced children who had not seen their father since he had been taken away three years earlier to a reeducation camp; and lovely seventeen-year-old Laon who had braved storms and pirates to follow her young fiancé; and the laughing student Qung and his nine young friends who had more bailed than sailed their way in a leaky boat to Hong Kong.

Of some, like Lan the fisherman, I wondered if they could ever laugh again. When twenty-year-old Uoc's boat capsized in a storm, he clung to a plastic container for two and a half days, and then he was rescued by a ship, given a meal, and cast away again into the sea on a crude raft, to be washed ashore another two days later. My, a fourteen-year-old boy, was one of the six survivors of a party of teenagers who drifted across the South China Sea for five weeks, feeding on seaweed in an open boat with a sail made from a shirt and a pair of jeans. Banh escaped by swimming two and a half miles to safety when over a hundred people were massacred by the Vietnamese garrison at Pugad, an island in the South China Sea. Ki's boat was attacked by pirates, who killed fifteen passengers and made off with five young girls.

The office of the UN High Commissioner for Refugees told me about Tran Hue Hue (pronounced Hwai Hwai). Though they could give me only the bare details, I knew at once that this was a story I must write if only to show how this young girl had survived an unimaginable ordeal.

In order to find out more about Hue Hue I went, by way of

the Philippines, first to a remote island of fisherfolk, then to the refugee camps on Palawan Island and in Manila. I continued my journey to Malaysia—to Kuala Lumpur, Trengganu, and Pulau Bidong, the boat people's island camp—until I came to East Hills, a Sydney suburb and the government hostel, where I found Hue Hue. The person I saw before me was a young Chinese girl, sturdily built and rather short, with a mischievous but highly intelligent expression in her eyes. She looked so bright and fresh in her flowery, short-sleeved cotton dress and sandals that I found it hard to believe this little girl had managed to survive the ordeal of Ladd Reef.

Hue Hue led me to the small ground-floor apartment where I was to talk to her and her father, Tinh, her mother, Le Mai, and her brothers Quang and To. I very soon felt tremendous affection for this charming, hospitable family who were so patient and helpful. We sat around on a bed or a chair in one of the two bedrooms for hours and hours, day after day, while I gathered my story. Hue Hue gave up her days off from school, and on schooldays came home at 4:30 P.M. to talk with me till midnight or later. I occasionally helped her with her homework—I remember once it was the story of Cinderella—but that was small recompense for the long hours that she and her father put in on my behalf. I am deeply grateful to them for this and for allowing me to write the story of Tran Hue Hue. I have from time to time had to use my imagination to piece it together, but I believe that my interpretation is a true reflection of the sympathy, admiration, and affection I feel for this family, representatives as they are of all the boat people.

1

In the early 1960s there lived in South Vietnam a young couple, Luong Tinh and his wife, Le Mai. Their home was in Cantho, a busy city on the delta of the great Mekong River, southwest of the capital, Saigon.

Tinh and Le Mai, though Vietnamese by nationality, were both Hoa, ethnic Chinese, by birth. They grew up in a country that had belonged to the French empire for over half a century. Vietnam, a long thin country, has as its northern neighbor China, which seems on the map to sit heavily on its head. To the west, Laos and Cambodia (Kampuchea) have squeezed it into a narrow strip against the South China Sea, which washes the whole length of Vietnam's 1,250-mile eastern coast from near Hanoi, the northern capital, to Saigon and the Mekong delta in the south.

Though European traders and missionaries first appeared in Vietnam in the first half of the sixteenth century, it was not until the seventeenth century that the French started missions there.

In the mid-nineteenth century, the subjugation of Vietnam began. By 1887 the northern province of Tonkin, with Annam in the center and Cochin China in the south, as well as

Cambodia, were all under the sway of France in what the latter called the Indochinese Union. Laos was added six years later.

The Vietnamese are a strong, nationalistic people. During the twentieth century, Vietnam's resistance to the French imperialists steadily increased. At the end of the thirties, when Luong Tinh was born and the world was drifting toward war, an organized resistance movement began. Its leader was living in exile in China. Born in 1890 with the name Nguyen That Thanh, he was to become known the world over as Ho Chi Minh, "The Brilliant One."

Ho had been expelled from school, had worked in a French liner as mess-boy, and in London as a kitchen hand. He found work in a photographic studio and as a dock-hand in Paris and was there when the Russian revolution broke out in 1917. Joining the French Communists, he founded in exile the Communist Party of Indochina in 1930. When the French Vichy government surrendered to the Nazis in 1940, allowing the Japanese to occupy bases in Vietnam, Ho Chi Minh turned up in Yunnan province in southern China. There he became leader of the Viet Minh, a force of Vietnamese partisans based in Yunnan who were fighting against both the Japanese invaders and the French imperialists across the border in Vietnam. Once World War II was over, Ho proclaimed himself president of the Independent Republic of Vietnam. But in 1946 the French were back, and though they and Ho came to terms, the Viet Minh kept up the fight.

Luong Tinh and Le Mai were still too young and too far away in their homes in the south to remember these events. They proved to be the curtain raiser to more than a quarter-century's war that was to devastate Vietnam, kill millions, and eventually lead to the exodus of the boat people, most of whom were not yet born.

Ho Chi Minh and his Viet Minh took to the villages and rice fields. Helped by their comrades across the border in Communist China, the Viet Minh guerrillas fought the French, until they defeated them decisively in 1954 at Dien Bien Phu. In July of that year, at Geneva, international statesmen decided for the time being to split the long, thin country along the 17th parallel into North and South. The mentality and the economy of the two halves differed essentially, the North being frugal, austere, and Communist, the South easygoing and capitalist.

The United States then called on the South to make a stand along the 17th parallel against the communism of the North. With American backing, Ngo Dinh Diem, a fervent Catholic and anti-communist, installed himself at Saigon as head of the South's regime. Using money and equipment supplied by the United States, he created a powerful army and a secret service, the Can Lao, headed by his brother, Nhu.

The Viet Minh decided to fight back against the aloof and autocratic Diem. They were joined by other elements that united under the banner of the National Liberation Front, whose aim was to drive out both Diem and the Americans. As enemies of the Saigon regime in the South, the government lumped them together with the Viet Minh under one contemptuous name—Viet Cong, short for Vietnam Cong San, or Vietnamese Communists.

In 1959, Luong Tinh was twenty-one, Le Mai a pretty seventeen. Le Mai lived in Cholon, the Chinese suburb of Saigon, and was therefore at the center of events. Neither she nor Tinh, whose home was in Cantho, some one hundred miles distant in the Mekong delta, were much worried by politics. They were young, in love, and thinking of marriage. Tinh had finished high school but instead of going on to college he apprenticed himself to a master watchmaker.

Tinh and Le Mai, both devout Buddhists of the Phat Giao sect, were married amid the solemnity, the color, and the clanging gongs of the Buddhist ritual. They settled in a one-story wooden house that Tinh had rented near the Ninh Kieu marketplace. In a small shop nearby, Tinh, with his newly acquired skill and his savings, started up his own business selling and repairing watches and clocks. His watches and spare parts were imported from Switzerland, Hong Kong, and Japan. His alarm clocks came from Red China. Watch straps and sunglasses completed his stock-in-trade. Tinh and his young bride left home on their motor scooter early every morning. They opened shop at seven, closing in the evening at five. Tinh's skill and his easy way with people brought him many customers. He and Le Mai began to prosper. "Life was good," he remembered. "There were no restrictions and we got a fair reward for our hard work."

Meanwhile, their thoughts were on another matter, one of capital importance to them and hardly less to their parents—the primordial duty of begetting a son to assure the succession. It was not long before Le Mai broke the good news to her husband: she was expecting a child. The baby was born the following year, 1960—a boy, Tran Dieu Trung. His birth was the happiest event ever in the life of Tinh and Le Mai—a son and heir at the first attempt.

Trung's birth called for a great family celebration, which took place in the nearby home of Le Mai's mother, Ngu Hong, their own house being too small to receive the one hundred or so guests. Everyone wished well for little Trung, and was glad for his young parents.

Amid the family rejoicings, gloomy political events were forgotten, though one of considerable importance took place that year: the establishment in Saigon of a U.S. military command with its thousands of "technicians." The South was now ablaze against the Saigon regime. In the forefront of the militants protesting against the tyranny of the brothers Diem and Nhu were the Buddhists. In the squares of Saigon and other cities Buddhists bonzes and nuns were going up in the smoke and flames of their self-made funeral pyres. The burnings helped to hasten the downfall of America's nominee Diem. At the end of 1963 he and Nhu were assassinated by men of their own army. The United States, which had been solidly behind them, was now left with a war on its hands. The Americanization of the conflict began.

Tinh was a natural optimist, his young wife less so, but both remained undeterred by the signs of war from their determination to increase their family. In March 1964 their next child was conceived. Tinh's watchmaking business continued to prosper, and while Le Mai's hands were too full with the baby Trung to help in the shop, her brother Hien, a watch repairer himself, came in to help Tinh. It was lucky he did so, for in November Tinh, now twenty-six, was called up and attached to the U.S. cipher office in Cantho. He could hardly complain, for the war was still far away and his home close. He could go back home every night.

Then in December, came a new crisis in the form of another military coup. Eight days later, on December 28, Le Mai went into labor. Tinh hurried on his Vespa to the hospital, a private one woefully lacking in modern equipment. All went well, however, and Tinh was informed that he was the father of a beautiful girl.

It was all he desired. His succession assured by Trung, he had longed for a girl. Le Mai felt the same; she had already chosen a girl's name, Hue Hue, which is depicted by the Chinese character meaning magnificent lily. Tinh agreed; the name was a sign of their hopes for the future. Though times might be unsettled, they prayed that the flower would blossom and multiply and give fruit.

Hardly had Hue Hue opened her eyes on the small world around her than far away in Saigon, yet another military coup brought a further change of government. The Buddhists, finding these fleeting regimes no less odious than Diem's, continued to perform their fiery human sacrifices in the squares of Saigon. As little Hue Hue grew plump and strong, the black, nauseating smoke of the bonzes' burnt offerings, rising into the sky, marked the way to the holocaust in which the whole of Vietnam would one day be engulfed.

The Americanization of the war was well under way. U.S. Marines landed at Da Nang, just south of the 17th parallel. President Johnson declared America's full support for South Vietnam and its president, General Thieu.

Meanwhile, thousands of the South's helicopters, rotor blades rhythmically thumping the air, flew ceaselessly to and fro across the countryside, while the South's bombers, in their efforts to discover Viet Cong hideouts and destroy the crops off which they fed, sprayed poisonous defoliants over forests and flowers and fields of standing rice, stripping them bare. Elsewhere, more and bigger bombers—B-52s—and warships of the U.S. Sixth Fleet were blasting towns and villages of the North into rubble, killing, burning, and disfiguring thousands—most of them women and children. During these long and dreadful years, Vietnam, North and South, was devastated by aerial bombing and land battles. Little Trung and Hue Hue were spared most of these horrors.

Hue Hue was a precocious child. At eleven months she began to walk and talk—mostly to Trung, for the little boy made much of his sister, who in turn adored him. He could not bear being parted from her. When he was, she would ask for him by the name she had invented, Chung Co—Trung-brother. So began a devoted friendship between the two.

Towns like Cantho were as yet hardly touched by guerrilla warfare. In his off-duty hours, Luong Tinh managed to keep his business going with the precious help of his brother-in-law Hien. But only just. Whether he were to survive or be killed, the war threatened to ruin Tinh and his family. He had no particular feelings for the Thieu regime nor indeed against the North's, of which he knew little and cared less. He just longed for the end of the war and with it the end of American intervention. As optimistic as ever, Tinh believed that the American and South Vietnamese armies, with their vast apparel of war, must come out the winners, and sooner rather than later. So it was not surprising that Tinh had soon fathered another child. In June 1967, Le Mai presented him with a second son—Tran Dieu Quang, or Quang for short. With their mother busy with the new baby, Trung and Hue Hue began to depend still more on one another.

Hue Hue had just celebrated her third birthday, and the family was looking forward to Tet, the lunar new year. This year, 1968, it fell on January 29. On New Year's eve, called *Giao Thua*, the whole of Vietnam was on the move, with families gathering to pray the following day at the ancestral shrine, to feast and exchange presents.

But in the early hours of the twenty-ninth, the first day of Tet, as families were breaking up from the traditional "farewell to ancestors" dinner, the rattle of machine-gun fire and the crash of mortar shells made the people of South Vietnam, wherever they were, in villages, towns, and cities, realize that the Viet Cong were among them.

The struggle was growing fiercer; the Americans, for all their massive power, were unable to pin down or repel their determined, tenacious foes. It looked to President Johnson as if a military victory against the Viet Cong was impossible. Moreover, the war had become extremely unpopular in the United States. In May 1968, peace talks between the United States and North Vietnam opened in Paris.

Tinh had a feeling that the war would soon be over; he talked to Le Mai, raising a point that to him was very dear— that they should round out their family by adding one more child. Halfway through the summer Le Mai told him she was expecting another baby—due March 1969.

Tinh had further plans. The family had become a tight fit in their small rented house. Tinh had saved up enough money from his business and now he bought a bigger house in Cantho. Its three bedrooms, brick walls, tiled roof, glass windows, and solid front door with peephole were outward signs of Tinh's prosperity. He and Le Mai had their bedroom, and Hue Hue her own, with pictures of family and friends and her favorite actress, Chan Chan, on the pale blue walls. The two boys, Trung and Quang, slept in the third room—and slept comfortably, like the rest of the family, between the sheets that Tinh could now afford to buy.

With the peace talks on and a baby on the way, Tinh and his family looked hopefully to the future. But as the time approached for the birth of the new baby, even his optimism began to fade. Despite the Paris talks, there still was no sign yet of an end to the fighting. The Americans were withdrawing from Vietnam and the "Vietnamization" of the war had begun. The time came when the U.S. cipher office in Cantho closed down and all the Vietnamese working there, Tinh included, were sent up to the front to a combat unit.

Le Mai was left alone with her three small children while

12

she waited for her fourth—and for word from her husband. But no word came back; Tinh's unit was suffering heavy losses in the fighting, which allowed no respite for writing letters. Tinh was not unduly anxious for himself, but he worried for his wife and family. His death would mean the end of his business and leave them destitute. Le Mai was anxious and overworked, but kept him posted with the family news. Hue Hue and the boys often cried because their father was no longer with them.

Tinh at last received the message he had anxiously awaited. His company commander, a good friend, was nearly as pleased as Tinh by the news that Le Mai was about to give birth and told him, "Off you go, but get back as soon as the baby's born."

It was past midnight when a knock at the door of the house in Cantho awoke the family. Hue Hue was there first and through the peephole recognized her father, his rifle slung on his shoulder. She almost tore the door open, jumped into his outstretched arms, and with a squeal of delight hugged him. Tinh raised the little girl above his head, kissed her, and lowered her to the floor. Then it was the turn of Trung and Quang, who had been jumping with excitement. One by one, Tinh hugged them, patted them, and put them gently down again. Le Mai had been watching. He took her and embraced her tenderly, asking for the latest news. "You have come just in time," she told him. Next day, Tinh was at her side when she gave birth to a third boy; they had already chosen a name for him, Tran Dieu To, or just To. Tinh and Le Mai sensed a new balance in the family. Close as they all felt to one another, the children seemed to fall naturally into two groups: Trung and Hue Hue, who were already inseparable, and Quang and To, who would become so.

In the fleeting hours of Tinh's brief leave the war was

forgotten. Then, as abruptly as he had come, he left again for the front.

Though the peace talks had been dragging on in Paris for nearly two years, no glimmer of peace appeared. Hardly had Tinh reached his unit at the front when the fighting flared up. But U.S. forces were still being steadily withdrawn. For Ho Chi Minh, the American withdrawal was a partial victory, though he would not live long enough to see its fulfillment. He died on September 3, 1969.

Trung and Hue Hue were two of the smallest of the 1,300 pupils of the Tho Nhon High and Primary School of Cantho city. Dressed in the neat school uniform—a spotless white shirt and for Trung blue shorts, for Hue Hue a blue pleated skirt—they walked there hand in hand every day accompanied by their aunt Phuong or aunt Binh; still in her teens, Binh was a pupil at the High School. Soon the children learned to pick their way alone among the crowds and through the teeming traffic of Cantho. But never did Hue Hue let go the hand of Trung. He was her anchor and with him she felt safe. In the classroom they sat together. Hue Hue began the way all children do—drawing pictures, learning the names and shapes of trees and plants, of animals and birds, the commonest of them all being the seagulls that wheeled and glided above the Mekong delta.

Hue Hue had decided views on the animals in her life. Her liking for dogs went no further than the family dog and its daughter. Oddly enough, both were called Dolly. Hue Hue saw to it that neither Dolly succumbed to the fate of many Vietnamese dogs—to be cooked and eaten at Christmastime. The fact that her father kept two pigs that were being fattened for the same purpose did not upset Hue Hue in the least. She hated pigs, but pork was another thing. She hated too the lizards that ran up and down the walls inside the house; they frightened her and she refused to believe her father when he teased her, saying that they brought the house good luck.

When she was six, Hue Hue moved to primary school. Her teacher was Huynh My, whose husband Hun Hinh taught in the secondary school at Tho Nhon. Hue Hue's aunt Binh was one of his best pupils; but it was soon clear that Huynh My and Hue Hue did not get along. "She was rather a mischievous little girl," Huynh My later commented in a disapproving voice. Hue Hue, whose native tongue was Cantonese, had to learn the official Chinese dialect, Mandarin, as well as Vietnamese. "Hue Hue often did her homework badly," continued Huynh My, "and the next day I had to punish her." Five strokes of a ruler on the knuckles. "I don't think she minded in the least, she never cried," Huynh My recalled, rather frustrated by her defiant little pupil, who she summed up as lazy and not particularly intelligent. Yet Hue Hue was to prove that her energy and intelligence were far greater than was needed to make the top of her class at Tho Nhon.

Her brother Trung was differently made—a quiet, serious boy, good at his lessons, especially math. It was already apparent that his reactions were logical, while Hue Hue's were instinctive and impulsive. Together they made a fine team.

Fervent Buddhists, Le Mai and Tinh took good care to hand on to their children a basic religious teaching. As a seven-year-old, Hue Hue understood this to mean that she must be kind to all people and help those in need, harm neither people nor animals, lead a moral life, and not be greedy. This last precept was the hardest for her, for Hue Hue had a robust appetite. Often on the way home from school she would persuade Trung to buy sweets and cakes; there were so many street vendors about, the temptation was too great. She went twice a month to the temple with her parents and brothers, bringing offerings of food and fruit and flowers. These seemed to her reasonable compensation for the sweets and cakes she had devoured.

So Le Mai and Tinh brought up their children to worship the Lord Buddha, to have faith in God. They were taught, too, to love and obey their parents and respect their elders. Admittedly Hue Hue's grandfather, her mother's father, spoiled her, but how could the old man help it when his small granddaughter was so attentive to him? When he came to the house at the end of a hot and busy day, she would help him off with his shoes and bring him sandals; with a bamboo lath she would soothe his itching back and when it ached, massage it, pummeling the tired muscles with her solid little fists.

While the Paris talks seemed to go on interminably, for the suffering people of Vietnam the war continued. Hue Hue and Trung often talked about their father. They both worried about him and, with the rest of the family, prayed daily for his safety. Occasionally Tinh would turn up unexpectedly. Hardly had he time to unsling his rifle and put it aside than Hue Hue and Trung were in his arms, while Quang and To fingered the rifle admiringly. When their father was at home, Hue Hue and Trung would always run back from school—no stopping for sweets—and there would be a meal in their grandparents' home to celebrate. Afterward, the whole family would visit the temple, laying their offerings at the feet of the Buddha, then bowing in prayer, imploring protection, especially for Tinh.

The war still dragged on until in 1972 the North launched a new offensive against the South. Immediately the U.S. air force was brought back into action. Never in the history of aerial warfare had so great a tonnage of bombs been dropped as that which fell over Indochina. The air raids drew closer and closer to Cantho.

Next door to Tinh and Le Mai's house was a hospital. One day Trung, noticing that people were thronging around the entrance, became curious. Taking Hue Hue by the hand he slipped through the crowd and into the hospital. The children recoiled aghast at the sight that met their eyes: soldiers and civilians, victims of the bombing, many of them boys and girls like them, lay in disorder on the floor, their clothing in shreds, their bodies stained with blood, mutilated, decapitated. Momentarily, Hue Hue felt compassion for these poor, shattered people. Then the horror of the scene struck her. She tugged at Trung's hand and they slipped through the crowd and away. Neither of them could sleep that night. It was the first time they had come face to face with death. At long last, in October 1972 in Paris, the United States and Hanoi agreed on a cease-fire. By March, all American troops had left the country.

With the cease-fire, Corporal Tinh could get home more often and for longer. He had been at the front for four years; his unit had fought hard and suffered heavy casualties, once narrowly escaping being wiped out when it fell into a Viet Cong ambush.

Though Tinh had been present daily in the prayers of his wife and children at the family shrine, they had never really learned to live without him. Now that they were all together again, it was a time for rediscovering the happy days of long ago. Le Mai and Tinh meant everything to one another, and their four children were a treasure far more precious to them than the wealth they had lost because of the Communist offensive. Never must they lose the children to communism too. "They were very loving and obedient children," said Tinh. "We always did things together and if anyone wanted to stay at home, we all stayed." Quang and To had become the closest of friends; Trung and Hue Hue still were.

By 1974 the two older children moved up into the high school at Tho Nhon. Hue Hue's horizon began to widen. She was learning physics and chemistry. Through geography and history she was gaining knowledge of the world far beyond Cantho and of historical figures other than Thieu and Ho Chi Minh (about whom—or whose ideas—the general public in the South was not at present overly concerned). Hue Hue, in any case, was never bothered by things or people beyond her immediate circle. She was a practical girl; her father had a successful business again, and when she could she helped in his store. Trung helped too, but it was Hue Hue who had the hardest head for business.

Hue Hue loved to please her parents. One of the surest ways was to cook for them. Tinh, more than anyone, appreciated Hue Hue's cooking. With his approval she invited her friends Le Trinh and Hoa to the house on weekends, for cooking sessions. No boys were invited, because in Vietnam boys were not supposed to be interested in cooking. Her brothers were something of an exception; their parents encouraged them to help their sister and they enjoyed it.

So each weekend Hue Hue had a free hand in the kitchen; she was as skillful at frying as at steaming fish, chicken, and pork, the basic favorites; she regaled the family with rice cakes, sponge cakes, and all kinds of other good things like *banh khot*, a pancake filled with pork, prawns, and bean sprouts.

Aside from cooking, Hue Hue took pleasure in many activities, both alone and with her family. The doll she owned interested her less than the clothes she made for it: she became an expert seamstress. But she was as happy out of doors as in. Her energy was unbounded. Up at five o'clock in the morning, she would go bicycling with her friends and brothers; often her father, too, would join them. Everyone in the family owned a bicycle—except To, who was still struggling with the family tricycle on which all the children had learned. Small, agile, and athletically built, Hue Hue was often first past the tape in races at school. At table tennis she would beat most comers, though Trung was her equal.

Of all her friends, Trung was the one she loved the most. He was always helpful and attentive with both her and her young brothers. It was he who taught her to dance, he who most often took her to the movies on the back of his Honda. One day, without his knowing, she tried the Honda out alone; it was the only time she could remember Trung being angry with her, and even then he was no more than mildly annoyed.

During the holidays the family would go by coach to the seaside at Vung Tau. Hue Hue loved the water, though she was not a strong swimmer. Trung never learned to swim.

The cease-fire signed in 1972 was being repeatedly violated. Behind the uneasy truce, Hanoi had been preparing the *coup de grâce*.

Tinh was recalled to the front a few weeks before the North launched its great offensive in April 1975. In mid-April he came home on forty-eight hours' leave. As usual the children were around his neck hugging him, but Le Mai noticed immediately that his customary smile was gone; he looked tired, his manner was grave. The North's offensive was gaining ground so rapidly that as their troops closed in on Saigon, the roads were choked with refugees fleeing toward the capital.

People in Cantho, though, still seemed to be going about their lives as if no war existed. Yet the South's army, Tinh told Le Mai, was on the verge of collapse. Before he left, Tinh gathered Le Mai and the children around him and told them: "I cannot say when I shall be back again, but keep praying for me." Then, after embracing them one by one, he was gone. That night they all lit joss sticks at the family shrine and prayed. They cried, because they were afraid for him, now more than ever. Hue Hue believed that God would protect him.

Two weeks later, on April 30, the North's armored units and infantry swept into Saigon. The war was all but over. A few days later Hue Hue, with her mother and brothers, was among the crowd that watched silently as the *bo doi*, the soldiers of the North, came marching into Cantho in green uniforms and sun-helmets, their Russian rifles held at the hip. The family all shared the same fear, not because of the *bo doi*, but for their father. There had been no word from Tinh since he left.

2

Following the Communist takeover—it was at first hailed in the South as a "liberation"—people waited expectantly, wondering what would happen. The *bo doi* lost no time in hanging out banners that carried such slogans as: "There is nothing more precious than independence and freedom," "Our great president Ho still lives in our hearts," "Long live the people and the army, united to build socialism." There was no mention of communism—only of democracy, reconciliation, and national unity. Very soon prices rocketed; rice, for example, rose from 80 to 500 piasters a kilo, gasoline from 200 to 1,600 piasters a liter. The main target for the North's "new culture" was the capitalist, yet God-fearing, culture of the South. Christian churches, most of them Roman Catholic, were closed, as were Buddhist temples of the Cao Dai and Hoa Hao sects, both violently anti-Communist. Though the Phat Giao, Tinh's sect, was spared, feasting and celebrations were forbidden. It was also forbidden to bring any but the most modest offerings to the temple. Chicken, the usual one, was in any case almost unobtainable and exorbitantly expensive.

The South's daily newspapers disappeared from the streets, to be replaced by government dailies: *Giai Phong* ("Freedom"), and later *Tin Sang*, published by the Patriotic Front. All bookshops were forced to close down and their stock was seized; books available under the old regime, even those of the most celebrated authors, both national and international, were considered decadent. Private houses were raided, their owners' libraries confiscated or burned. Cinemas no longer showed European and American movies but instead educational and often boring propaganda films from Russia or China. No pretext was accepted for walking out before the end of the show—that would be an insult to the "new culture."

The new culture came pouring forth, too, from the transmitters of Radio Saigon. Broadcasts were no longer sauced with the songs and music of the capitalist world but with wordless music. Other aspects of capitalist decadence were dealt with similarly. Schools, universities, and other seats of bourgeois learning were closed. Squads of the Patriotic Youth, armed with scissors, stationed themselves at important crossroads and clipped the heads of long-haired youngsters. The ends of their bell-bottomed jeans were cut off too, and if they wore an open-neck shirt, they were ordered to button it up.

If the North imposed its new culture so aggressively on the South, the South's old culture, condemned by the North as worn out, rotten, and capitalist, nevertheless easily seduced its conquerors' unwary soldiers and officials. They lost no time in laying their hands on tempting consumer goods unknown to them in the spartan North—cars and motorcycles, cameras, and watches—paying inordinately high prices for them.

At the end of May the schools reopened. So far Hue Hue, Trung, and their two small brothers had not come up against any problem with the new culture. Avant-garde clothes and hairdos were not their style. Their education, both at school and under the watchful eyes of their parents, had been thoroughly conventional. It had made them honest, God-fearing, and happy children who loved and respected their father and mother as they did one another. They were a solid bourgeois family. But now, as four of the millions of "nieces" and "nephews" of Uncle Ho, it was as if they were being adopted into a new and strange family. All the former teachers had been fired or sent to reeducation camp, to be replaced by teachers from the North. Hue Hue's political teacher was very strict and, listening to his outpourings, she and Trung, Quang, and To began to feel that they were no longer brothers and sister, nor the children of their father and mother, but that Uncle Ho was their only parent and only to him must they look. Schoolchildren were persuaded, too, to pray not to the Lord Buddha, nor for that matter to the Lord Jesus Christ, but only to Uncle Ho who, though dead these six years, was still among them.

Indoctrination started as soon as a child could reasonably absorb it. For older children like Trung, who was nearly fourteen, and even for his youngest brother, six-year-old To, it was more a matter of brainwashing—two hours a day with an occasional visit of the entire school to a local seminary to listen to a *can bo*, an official, lecturing for the best part of a day on Uncle Ho and the blessings he had brought to the people. At first the children took it all as rather a joke. Uncle Ho became the butt of their rhymes and their funny stories. But the joke began to wear thin as more and more Communist propaganda was drilled into their young heads. To be told to respect their own parents less than Uncle Ho worried and offended children who had been brought up to honor their father and mother. Of Tinh's family, Trung, the most sensitive of the four, was the most upset. He told his father that he was disgusted and demoralized, that he had little heart left to attack his normal work that till now had so absorbed him. Hue Hue, more down to earth, treated the brainwashing with contempt. As for Quang and To, most of it went clean over their heads. They hardly knew what to make of the Uncle Ho line and found it very boring—quite as boring as the two-hour periods that all the pupils were forced to spend every few days sweeping and cleaning the streets or weeding and watering the flower beds in the public gardens. Hue Hue had no enthusiasm for gardening. It was for later, perhaps when she was an old lady, she thought.

The new rulers from the North had spread word in their propaganda that they would seize the wealth of the rich and share it out among the poor. In the South, much of the wealth lay in the hands of astute, hardworking Chinese, and the effect of the propaganda was to spread resentment among Vietnamese against the Chinese. Tinh was well known in Cantho as a man of some affluence; at school Hue Hue began to notice that her friends no longer wanted to talk and to play with her. Then, unexpectedly, something far more sinister happened. One evening when all the children were home from school, two policemen wearing the new yellow uniform called at the house. First they handed Le Mai a letter; she immediately recognized Tinh's handwriting and tore it open. Tinh wrote briefly that he was well. Fighting on with his unit after the fall of Saigon, he had been captured, taken to a reeducation camp—he did not say where—and told that he would be released after a month. That, reckoned Le Mai, would be the beginning of June.

For a moment, as she told the children about their father, Le Mai forgot her fear of the police. The children, who also had been very frightened, managed a shout of joy. Then one of the policemen spoke. "I have orders to search the house," he said gruffly. Quang and To, eyeing his automatic rifle, thought it looked far more menacing than their father's. The policemen proceeded to go through all the rooms, then left half an hour later, telling Le Mai, "We shall be back." Their words left no impression on Le Mai. She hardly heard them. The news that her husband Tinh was still alive and would soon be home effaced all the unpleasant, frightening things; she and the children talked about nothing else until they went to bed. Mercifully, they had no idea of what went on in the reeducation camps.

The "candidates" for reeducation—men who had served the Saigon regime in the forces, the police, and the administration, as well as professional men—were informed that their course would vary from a few days to a month, according to their rank or the importance of their post. But thousands of them are still waiting to be released—unless they are already dead.

It was some time before anything seeped out about the camps. But when it did, horrifying stories reached the ears of anxious, waiting families. A typical course of reeducation began in Camp 7709 near Long Giao, sixty miles east of Saigon—a place especially reserved for the most recalcitrant anti-Communists.

The discipline was unrelenting. During the first four months the curriculum consisted of ten "lessons." The first five lessons were a condemnation of American imperialism and of its puppet, the Saigon government. Lesson six listed the enemies of the Communist government—in general, all who were imprisoned for reeducation. The Buddhist statues in the south, however, were also included. At times the prisoners felt like laughing out loud, but they did not dare or they would have been pushed outside and left standing under the blazing sun.

Lesson seven was tedious: each prisoner had to write his *so yeu lilich*, his curriculum vitae, in which he confessed that he had been an enemy of communism and deserved to be punished. The *so yeu lilich* was a dangerous snare, for repeated versions were demanded and each one compared for errors and omissions.

"The Communist party of Vietnam respects human rights," was the theme of lesson eight. "It has no wish to kill any of its enemies in Vietnamese society, but only to reeducate them so that they become good Communists." Lessons nine and ten labored the point further: "Only by hard labor can the state enemy's brain be washed clean so that he becomes a good Communist."

After some time many of the prisoners could stand the brainwashing no longer and, in despair, hanged themselves. Malnutrition—in particular the lack of vitamin B, which provoked skin diseases, beriberi, and edema and left them half-starved—added to the rows of graves outside the camp.

Four months after their arrival, prisoners were transferred to a camp at Tan Hiep. Here, too, they died by the score through lack of nourishment and medicine. Those who survived were sorted out. "Hard" cases—paratroopers, marines, rangers, security men, fighter pilots, and a number of doctors and naval officers—were loaded at gunpoint into trucks and driven to the North, a one-way journey for most of them.

Lessons nine and ten of the curriculum—"Only by hard labor can be the brain be washed clean"—took place in a camp in the mountainous Mui Gia Map region, thirty miles east of Saigon, an area notorious for malaria and dysentery. The saying went, "*Ba Ra di de. Kho ve*"—"To get to Ba Ra is easy, but it is hard to get back." A few did, after fifteen months spent at gunpoint, hacking through the bush and the bamboo, felling trees in the jungle until the mountainside was bald. Then it was ready to cultivate. This they did by hand, planting corn, rice, and manioc.

Prisoners in the reeducation camps slept on the bare ground, rose before dawn, worked until after dusk. Anyone attempting to escape was shot, or worse. At Tan Hiep one morning, two officers made a dash for it. One got away, the other was wounded by a prison guard as he struggled to free his shirt, which had caught on the barbed wire. Six prisoners were ordered to carry the wounded man to the dispensary, where they were ordered: "Report here tomorrow at six." At the dispensary next morning, they found what one of them called a blood bag—"a kind of canvas bag. It had no human form at all, but was drenched with blood." "We carried it away," said one of them, "still dripping with blood and buried it outside the camp."

Oblivious of such horrors, Le Mai and the children waited impatiently for the return of Tinh. Even if life in the future was to be much harder, they would at least be together again, the happy family they used to be.

June came and with it another visit from two policemen. They asked no questions, but as before had "orders to search the house," which they did, taking notes now and then. Then they departed without a word, leaving Le Mai and the children perplexed and anxious. Their anxiety grew as the days went by into mid-June and on to the end of the month with no sign of Tinh. Anxiety turned into despondency, for rumors were now beginning to spread about the reeducation camps. But the family, most fervently Hue Hue, kept hoping and praying daily at the household shrines for Tinh's safe return.

One day early in August, a haggard figure, his clothes hanging loosely on him, stood at the door. It was Tinh, and there was a thin smile on his face. He held his arms out as he always did, and the children, somewhat hesitantly, ran toward him, hardly believing. One after another they shyly embraced him. Tinh took Le Mai's hand. "Now it's over," he said to her. "We must never again be separated. Whatever may happen we must always stay together, all of us." While they talked, Hue Hue went to work, to cook. This time they dared not celebrate as in the old days, for that might have attracted the notice of the police, who, Tinh was well aware, would from now on be keeping a close eye on him.

A junior officer, Tinh had been released because his reeducation was considered complete. It might have been far worse. Like most people, he had found the political indoctrination unconvincing and sometimes comic; but though his brain remained unwashed by Communist dogma, he took careful note of what the government expected of its reeducated citizens. More than three months' forced labor, dawn to dusk, with an occasional blow on the back from a *bo doi*'s baton, had certainly told on him. But Tinh was resilient; his "reeducation" had been a salutary lesson for the future. In his mind, as in most people's, the war had been a fratricidal one. He had nothing against the Northerners as such. But about the new culture, about communism, he harbored no illusions. Life under the new regime was going to be miserable, especially for the onetime "enemies" of the state who, although they regained their civic rights on release from the reeducation camps, had lost practically everything else—including, for most of them, the desire to go on living in Vietnam.

Tinh's misgivings were confirmed when the police delivered a written order to him the day after his return. Curtly, it told him that he was forbidden to carry on his private business. He had expected as much; it was part of the government's anticapitalist campaign. But he was badly shaken when, two weeks later—at 8 P.M., after the curfew had fallen—a young lieutenant with a squad of *bo doi* came to the house and announced that he had orders to confiscate Tinh's entire stock. While his bewildered and frightened family looked on, Tinh was escorted to his shop. There the soldiers, directed by a man from the *cong an*, the criminal police, went to work carefully taking an inventory of every object. They found watches, bracelets, and sunglasses, as well as the expensive precision tools and spare parts vital to his trade. They searched everywhere, even under the floorboards, but did no damage. A guard was placed on the shop and Tinh was allowed to go home, with orders to be back at 8 P.M. the following evening. He was there on time and with a heavy heart watched as the *bo doi* cleared out the entire shop and loaded the proceeds into a truck. After emptying the shop, the *bo doi* boarded up the front door and windows, leaving a couple of men on guard. The prosperous livelihood that Tinh had built up with his skill and hard work during fourteen years had been demolished without trace in a few hours.

Tinh returned home. When he told Le Mai what had happened, she burst into tears. "I would rather kill myself now, this very minute," she sobbed, "than have our children taken away from us and turned into Communists." Of the children, only Trung and Hue had any idea of the disaster that had hit the family. But though they realized that their father had lost everything, they had yet to understand what, in material terms, that was going to mean to them.

Tinh, though ruined, was not the kind of man to accept defeat. He waited a week or so for things to calm down, then walked boldly into the district administrative office and asked to see the senior *can bo.* "*Kin thua bac,* I salute you, uncle," he began, using the usual expression of deference to a superior, who in this case was a young man, extremely unsure of himself before Tinh's disarming smile. Tinh asked politely if he might be accorded the favor of continuing to be useful to the community by practicing his trade at home, repairing watches. Even the best state watches needed overhauling from time to time, and Tinh, a master craftsman, was ready to serve the state. Permission was granted, and Tinh's equipment and tools—his delicate pincers, his tiny hammer and screwdriver, his eyeglass among them—were handed back to him.

Tinh now had work that provided a legitimate income—but far from enough to enable him to survive the huge increase in the cost of living. Food was short; chicken, fish, and pork, the family staples, were scarce and expensive. Forever short of liquid funds, Tinh asked leave of the district office to kill and eat his two fat pigs. The officials responded by ordering him to sell them forthwith to the government—at far below the market price. Tinh was hardly surprised, for he knew that it was the same the country over. Farmers were forced to sell their rice and fishermen their fish to the government, who paid well below the market price and resold to the public with an excessive profit.

Tinh bought another pig (on the black market, for trade in food and livestock on the open market was subject to government restrictions), but on short rations it refused to grow fat and Tinh had to sell it for a disappointing price. This time, however, Tinh was wiser. With Trung's help he took the unfortunate piglet around to a neighbor, who bought it. After the pigs, Tinh had to sell the furniture. Then Trung's Honda was sold. Since no more motor scooters were being imported it fetched a big price, but though that benefited the family kitty, it meant much less fun for Trung and Hue Hue. Not that it mattered, for their father could give then no more pocket money to go to the movies.

The main thing, however, was that Tinh was back in business. There was no lack of work, but with spares unobtainable he had to use all his skill in cannibalizing watches beyond repair to provide the bits and pieces to fit into less badly damaged ones. Tinh's keen eyes and sensitive hands remained as effective as ever. His repair business was not doing at all badly, but most of his profits went to the government in taxes.

Tinh, an honest man at heart, resolved to get even with the government. To a close friend he entrusted all the considerable savings he had amassed from the time he had started up in business. The new house he had bought had made a big hole in them, but Tinh still possessed a sizable fortune that he meant to keep intact in case times became too difficult. Besides these savings were his steadily growing profits from the watch-repair business, which he decided henceforth would not be declared to the government. With Tinh's cash savings, his friend bought gold bars on the black market; thanks to the "gradualism" practiced by Hanoi in socializing the South, the black market there was still rife—thanks not least to the corruption of government officials. Tinh's friend and he would meet casually in a *pho*, a bistro serving a popular dish of broth with noodles and sliced meat. In these days such places were little frequented and provided a secluded spot where the gold ingots could be slipped across to Tinh. Tinh was careful to change the next meeting place to another *pho*.

Tinh had to be very careful. While he had no reason to mistrust his neighbors—they were all in the same boat as he, hostile to the government—he could never be sure. He had to be realistic: in this police state even a friend or one of his children, bribed or brainwashed, might denounce him if he committed an imprudent act. For fear that the police might interrogate them, Tinh had to conceal his savings from his wife and children, except Trung, whose help he needed. Back at home, Tinh went to work, literally plowing his profits back into the soil. Around 9 P.M., well after curfew had fallen, he would grope his way down to the end of the garden, some fifteen yards from the house. There he would begin to dig. His tool was a trowel small enough to fit into his trouser pocket. While Trung kept watch, he dug a hole a foot deep in which he laid the gold bars, wrapped in a plastic bag. Then he covered them with earth and leaves. When he undertook these nocturnal excavations, Tinh always took a watering can with him. If Trung signaled danger, the police would find his father innocently watering the flowers.

The garden was not the only hiding place for Tinh's gold. In broad daylight, with two or three bars tied to his arm under his shirtsleeve, Tinh would climb the tall coconut tree that stood not far from the road. Sometimes passing friends would call to him, "Hey, Tinh, what are you doing up there?" and he would answer, "I'm after a few coconuts." He never failed to pick two or three and throw them down—but not before he had tied the gold bars firmly and invisibly to a cleft in the tree. Tinh did finally tell Le Mai what he was up to, but without revealing exactly where the gold was hidden. To the children, apart from Trung, he said nothing, for fear that the police might question them.

Thus Tinh, while managing to give the appearance of a poor, half-starved watch mender, was working overtime and secretly banking his gold bars. He felt certain that sooner or later he would need them.

The fourth Congress of the Vietnam Communist party met at Hanoi in December 1976. The premier, Pham Van Dong, announced that there would be a redistribution of Vietnam's work force in 1977. It would involve the resettlement of ten million Vietnamese and the reclamation of millions of acres of uncultivated land. As part of the plan, the government created New Economic Zones (NEZ for short), agglomerations of huts thrown together on poor, virgin land in remote parts of the countryside, mainly in the South. In a few NEZ's, bulldozers, trucks, and building materials, seeds, fertilizers, and a medical unit were provided, as well as a meager ration of coarse rice. At others the wretched settlers, though promised rice, received none; scratching away at the sparse soil, they looked more like skeletons clothed in rags. When no hand tools were available, the people had to fashion their own or work with their bare hands.

One purpose of the NEZ was the restructuring of society: dissidents and opponents of the regime could be dispersed and mixed with Northerners, themselves steeped in communism for the past twenty years.

All Vietnamese, but particularly townspeople, feared transfer to an NEZ as if it were a sentence of death—a slow, lingering death. It was the fate reserved for those viewed by the authorities as the dregs of Vietnamese urban society, for the penniless refugees who had flocked into Saigon and provincial cities at the end of the war, for prostitutes and vagabonds, for the onetime servants and hangers-on of the Saigon regime—in short, for everyone out of a job. The police possessed a simple means of forcing people to move to a NEZ—they simply confiscated their ration cards. Anybody classed as a capitalist, whose possessions had been confiscated, leaving him destitute, was ripe for an NEZ. There was no other possibility apart from death, or escape. Thousands of people were driven by the specter of the NEZ to choose this perilous alternative, escape.

Though Tinh had a job of sorts, his police record was against him: onetime owner of a private business, therefore ex-capitalist by definition, ex-soldier of the South's army, and at present impoverished watch mender working on his own. The thought that he and his family might end up in a NEZ weighed perpetually on his mind. As bad if not worse was the unbearable thought of their lovely children being converted forcibly to communism, being brought up in the Communist "faith," being taken from the family circle and placed under state tutelage. This would mean the breakup of the family.

Like countless thousands of his countrymen, Tinh was motivated to flee by more than material considerations. He might have stayed had not moral and religious considerations weighed so heavily. Well over half the boat people were women, teenagers, and children. To Tinh and Le Mai, as to other parents who fled Vietnam, the future of their children came before everything else. Parents too old or otherwise too tied down to leave urged their own children to do so.

Of the children, Trung and Hue Hue were naturally most affected by the changes in the school curriculum—the ceaseless indoctrination of Communist theory with its insidious purpose of weaning children away from their family and their faith. The hours spent in listening to propaganda and cleaning up the streets and public places interfered seriously with their normal studies. Trung, formerly so promising as a pupil, felt frustrated and depressed; the future looked empty to him, hardly worth living for. The ebullient Hue Hue was less affected, but even she was beginning to feel restless. The fun had gone out of life. She had talked to Trung about escaping and one day spoke to her father. "I have a friend who has a boat," she told him. "You must be patient," said Tinh. "We must wait a bit longer to see how things turn out."

Another consideration weighed still more heavily in the minds of Tinh and Le Mai. It concerned Trung. Slimly built, he looked older and was taller than most boys his age—as tall as his father and a good head taller than Hue Hue. Although Trung was only fifteen and below call-up age, Tinh and Le Mai were far from reassured. For the authorities, the size of the boy was more important than his age. As Tinh and Le Mai watched Trung grow up, they felt deepening affection for their son, whom Tinh later described as "a gentle boy. He kept clear of the little ruffians who fought each other in the street and never used their coarse language. He was very attached to his sister and his two young brothers and always took good care of them."

Trung was now more than ever the joy of his parents. Tinh and Le Mai agreed that at all costs their son must be saved from the call-up, spared from butchery perhaps in some future war against China (their own country, after all) or against Kampuchea. The press were saying that trouble was brewing with China over Kampuchea. For Trung's sake more than for any other reason, Tinh, by the end of 1976, became determined to escape with his family from Vietnam.

3

Some twenty years before the fall of Saigon, when Vietnam was divided in two following the defeat of the French at Dien Bien Phu, nearly a million refugees fled from North to South. Some of these escaped in boats and bamboo rafts. Though they were the first boat people, there was one main difference between them and their successors: these Northerners were moving from one part of their own country to another, not leaving it for good.

In 1975, when Saigon was captured by Communists, some 130,000 refugees were evacuated in landing craft and helicopters by the U.S. Sixth Fleet. They were running away from the reprisals they rightly feared the Communists would take against them for having worked with the Americans and the puppet government of President Thieu. They fled in panic for their lives.

Following the fall of Saigon, there began a new wave of refugees, motivated in a different way. They had waited to see how communism would work out, but having found it wanting in one essential—freedom—they refused to submit to the new regime. Their only alternative was to leave the country, forsaking all they possessed, their livelihood and their way of life, their homes and family ties and the ancestral tombs and urns—in short, everything that bound them to their beloved Vietnam. It is often asked how the boat people came to uproot themselves and make such a painful break with their past, why like people of other Communist countries they did not bow to the inevitable and accept the new order. Tinh had the answer: "We all agreed, my family and I, that we could not live under communism. We had lost our freedom. I could not stay and watch my children being turned into Communists, to die one day perhaps for our Communist rulers." And so many boat people have been heard to say, Tinh added: "Though I love Vietnam, rather than live there under communism I preferred to take the risk of dying at sea."

In a sense the boat people were acting in the same spirit as the Buddhist bonzes who, in the squares of Saigon, had deliberately burned themselves in protest against the tyranny of Diem and Thieu. The boat people too were quitting their Vietnamese world for another. They had faith; they believed that at their journey's end, wherever it might be, beyond the ocean or at the bottom of it, they would find a world better than the one they had left behind. The boat people were not simply running away; they were freedom fighters, though passive ones, striking a blow that cost them very dear, defending their rights as human beings.

The Thirteenth Article of the Universal Declaration of Human Rights plainly states: "Every person has the right to leave any country, including his own." The Hanoi government's answer to this, soon after the Communist takeover, was: "Those seeking to leave the country will be punished." That could mean being blown out of the water by a Vietnamese gunboat or, if recaptured, suffering a long term in a reeducation camp, followed probably by transfer for life to a New Economic Zone.

To most of these unhappy, rebellious subjects of the Hanoi

regime there was only one way of escape—the sea. The land routes to the west through Laos were barred by the Communist Pathet Lao; the Khmers Rouges of Communist Pol Pot controlled those through Kampuchea. A few Vietnamese did somehow get away by one or other of these ways to Thailand, but the best chance, if only little more than a fifty-fifty one, was to put to sea from somewhere along Vietnam's long coastline and steer for a foreign shore. The Thai coast is within 350 miles west or northwest of Ca Mau, the southernmost point of Vietnam. Nearer still, a bit west of south, is the coast of Malaysia, about 250 miles away. Farther south and twice the distance is Singapore; another 30 miles on across the Strait of Malacca, the swampy coast of Sumatra, Indonesia, shimmers in a hazy mirage rising off the glassy sea. Hong Kong was to become a refuge for boat people departing from the center or north of Vietnam. From the old capital Hue it was a voyage of some 700 miles, a bit less from Hanoi, the modern capital. Boat people bound for Hong Kong often traveled in slow-sailing junks, "coast crawling" off the shores of Hainan Island and the Chinese mainland and calling at Chinese ports for food and fuel. A slow boat to Hong Kong provided a relatively safe trip. Of all the sea routes the one eastward across the South China Sea to the Philippines was the most hazardous. Once past the shipping lanes of Vietnam there stretches for another 600 miles or so a desert of water, some of it the deepest water in the world, some the shallowest and most treacherous, where shifting currents and coral reefs abound.

All these routes suffer from a common hazard: the weather. Along the Hong Kong route, from July to September, the greatest peril comes from typhoons, with winds blowing up to 100 miles per hour and churning the sea into towering wave tops and gaping troughs. In October and November the full force of the typhoon season hits the South Vietnamese coast and the Philippines route. There is little risk of meeting typhoons on the routes to Thailand, Malaysia, and farther south. There the monsoon climate prevails, where winds blow up to gale force and stronger.

By the end of 1975 only a trickle of boat people—fewer than four hundred—had reached foreign ports or been picked up in mid-ocean. For a long time little was heard of them, though the remarkable exploits of some made news. It was entertaining reading, but it failed to shock the rest of the world into realizing that the curtain was rising on an appalling tragedy.

Non-communist countries of the Association of South-East Asiatic Nations (ASEAN) at this time showed no open hostility to the boat people. If offered permanent settlement in a "third country" like the United States or France the fugitives were sent on there to start a new life; otherwise their boat was resupplied and they were told to move on. One boat, the PK 504, left Cam Ranh bay in central Vietnam in mid-1976, only to meander from country to country through Southeast Asia for more than 5,000 miles before finally reaching Darwin, Australia.

By the end of 1976, the original trickle of boat people was increasing into a stream of over five thousand. Tinh had told Hue Hue, "We must be patient and see how things turn out." This was at first the view of most middle-class businessmen like Tinh, the main targets of the Communist doctrine: "With socialism [as the Hanoi government euphemistically called it], there is no private property. Everything belongs to the state." Early in 1977 Tinh had had enough of sitting at home mending watches. He began making plans to escape. When he told Le Mai, she was, as far as her reserved nature allowed, enthusiastic. Then suddenly she felt afraid. "But the *mat-vu*, the secret police, what if they find out?" "That," replied Tinh calmly, "is a risk we have to take. It is why I'm telling no one but you. Not a word to the children, but you must tell them that from now on they must always let you know where they're going and never go far from the house. When the time comes to leave we may have to get them together in a hurry."

Tinh had been able to form a broad picture of what escape involved. He had talked to a few trusted friends, and occasional guarded letters from relatives in California and Australia enabled him to get some idea of conditions there. Stories of the boat people were continually leaking through the grapevine and coming in over the BBC. Tinh's first choice of destination was Malaysia; it was nearest to Vietnam and more or less on the way to Australia, where he hoped eventually to settle, sponsored by Le Mai's cousin Ly To, who lived in Sydney. Another possibility was to sail first to Thailand, but Tinh was put off by rumors of piracy in the Gulf of Siam and by the problems of moving on to a third country. The Thai transit camps, he had heard, were overflowing with refugees from Laos and Kampuchea. He ruled out Singapore as an intermediate destination; it had the reputation of being the least sympathetic toward the boat people. As for Indonesia and the Philippines—why go all that far and run so many more risks? From the Mekong delta to Hong Kong was even farther. Tinh had never thought of escaping to China. Indeed, he laughed at the idea. "They are my people, it's true, but the trouble is, they are all Communists!"

Tinh's first escape attempt ended in dismal failure. He was as yet a novice at a dangerous and difficult game and paid a heavy price for his inexperience. A cousin of Tinh's had put him in touch with a boat owner. On the pretext of buying spare parts for his business, Tinh managed to get a permit to travel to Saigon; from there he pushed on to Vung Tau to discuss arrangements with the boat owner. The boat, a solid-looking craft built of wood, 80 feet long, 13 feet in the beam, and driven by a big four-cylinder diesel, reassured Tinh. "She'll carry more than a hundred passengers," said the owner. "For you and your family it will cost a kilo or so of gold. But all that you must fix up with the organizers."

The organizers were unknown to Tinh, but he had to trust them. His cousin introduced him one day in the street to a man with whom Tinh walked away as if casually chatting. In fact he was being told that, because there was government control on motor fuel, it was difficult to get enough. Some days later, they met again. This time the man told Tinh, "We now have all the diesel oil we need. Departure is set for April 20. I'll come around tomorrow to collect the gold."

Late that night when the rest of the family was asleep, Tinh, his trowel in his trouser pocket, crept out of the house and groped his way to the end of the garden. Silently he scraped away the earth covering his precious savings, then carried the gold bars back into the house and hid them under his mattress. Le Mai slept on.

Next morning, after the children had left for school, he climbed the coconut tree to recover the few gold bars hidden at the top, He did not forget to pick a couple of coconuts and throw them down to the ground, where Le Mai picked them up. Le Mai sensed that there might be something in the wind, but she never asked Tinh. She did not want to know for fear that the police might question her.

Later that morning the representative of the "organization" came, and Tinh handed him forty-two ounces in gold bars. Carefully the man distributed the gold among the deep pockets of his loose-fitting shirt and trousers. Then he left abruptly, with no more than "See you at Vung Tau on the twentieth."

As Tinh shut the door behind him, a sudden doubt flickered in his mind. The man of course had given him no receipt—to have done so would have provided evidence for the police that might have cost them both their lives. He had entrusted almost all his wealth to a man he had scarcely seen before and had no reason to trust.

Two days later Tinh heard an urgent knocking at the front door. It was his cousin. Hardly had Tinh let him in than the man stammered: "I've just heard that the police have discovered the boat. The trip's off." For days, anxiety gnawing at him more and more, Tinh waited for the man who had taken his gold; but of him and the other organizers he heard no more. They had disappeared.

Tinh turned again to repairing broken watches. Disheartened as he was, he felt more determined than ever to attempt another escape.

4

Tinh calculated that even if all went well, it would take him another year to put aside the extra gold that, added to his dwindling savings, he would need for the next attempt. The disappointment he felt at his costly failure was to some degree mitigated by the stories he heard about the boat people. Surreptitiously, he listened to the BBC World Service, his ear pressed against his transistor radio, whose volume was turned down to the minimum. It was a crime to listen to a foreign broadcast, and Tinh did not want even the children to know he was doing so; a chance remark to a school friend might give him away. The boat people's grapevine filled in the details. It was a worldwide and extraordinarily efficacious communications system for passing on information about the fugitives. News originated directly from the boat people themselves or was gleaned from the media—the "ethnic" press, radio, and TV. Messages circulated by cable, telephone, letter, and word of mouth among the refugees and between them and their friends and relatives inside and outside Vietnam. The messages brought good news and bad, as well as offers of sponsorship from émigré relatives. They not infrequently confirmed the whereabouts of families and friends separated en route by misfortune, storms, or pirates and who later could be reunited. Between them, the BBC and the grapevine gave Tinh an encouraging picture. Despite the mounting vigilance of the authorities and a host of other dangers, more and more people were escaping by boat.

But danger stalked from the moment the decision to leave was made. To be suspected of trying to escape was grounds enough for arrest. The fear of denunciation and discovery haunted the fugitives as they prepared, for the secret police had informers everywhere. No one could trust his neighbor, nor his friend; schoolchildren were encouraged to denounce their parents; fishermen were bribed to report on ship movements. Danger accompanied the refugees still more closely from the moment they closed the doors of their homes for the last time and made their way down to the remote creek or beach where the boat lay hidden. During the voyage these hardy seafarers (most of whom had never been to sea in their lives before), were in peril from naval patrols and pirates, from hunger and thirst, from storms and from sinking in their leaky boats when their laboring, unreliable engines broke down. If they were lucky enough to reach land, they could not even then be sure of finding refuge.

Tinh realized only too well that if it was hard to get out of Communist Vietnam and survive the voyage to a democratic country, getting into that country was likely to be just as difficult.

As the number of boats sailing away from Vietnam grew into an armada, the rest of the world reacted, not with sympathy but with a hardening of heart against the boat people. Vietnam's closest neighbors had domestic problems of their own, which an influx of refugees could only aggravate. Thailand's refugee camps were overflowing with fugitives from

Laos and Kampuchea, and the pleas of the Thais to the wealthy industrial nations to help in settling them were unheard save by a few. Singapore flatly refused to allow the boat people to land unless they could show proof that a welcome awaited them in a "third" country, foremost among which were the United States and France. Canada, Australia, and Malaysia (which accepted only Muslims) were the only other countries at this time to have taken in more than a thousand refugees. So, having survived a perilous, exhausting voyage, they were either detained indefinitely under armed guard aboard their small boats or, if the boats were judged seaworthy, given supplies and ordered to move on—seldom knowing where they'd end up. Some crept on down the coast, scuttled their boats, and camped out on the beach; a few sailed on to Indonesia, or farther to Australia. A few more made the risky voyage to the Philippines.

Survivors picked up by merchant ships at sea and taken to the next port of call were treated like the rest. Hundreds of others, despite their distress signals, were left to their fate. Shipping companies were held responsible for the survivors they rescued, and many companies, to save money, were base enough to instruct their captains not to stop for the boat people. Old men and women, young men and girls, children and babies drowned before the pitiless gaze of the merchantman's captain and crew, or drifted in their foundering craft out of sight.

Toward the end of 1977, Thailand's camps held nearly 100,000 Indochinese refugees from Kampuchea, Laos, and Vietnam. The Thai government decided that the time had come to push the refugees back across Thailand's land frontiers. At sea, Thai naval patrols went into action; the boat people, driven farther south, converged on Malaysia. There too the government got tough and began to repel by force the invasion from the sea.

To the wealthy countries and Western democracies, which cried shame at such inhuman treatment, the Asian countries concerned responded, "You won't take them, so why should we?" As if any individual or nation, from East or West, had the right to refuse help to the helpless, especially to those in peril at sea!

The behavior of the wealthy nations, the consumer societies gorged with food and freedom, was disgraceful. In Vietnam, where human freedom and dignity were being treated with contempt, suffering, believing people were braving death in freedom's name. But countries that loudly proclaimed their defense of freedom and human rights were now turning their backs on the refugees who came from the sea. "Sink the boat people." That phrase, chalked on a walk in a Sydney suburb, summed up the callousness of other nations. The boat people were beginning to realize that the rest of the world did not want them. And yet they kept coming, over 20,000 of them by the end of 1977. A nearly equal number perished at sea. Almost 80,000 "enemies" of the regime were locked up in the jails of Ho Chi Minh City (Saigon's new name). It was an augury of the exodus to come.

5

Outside the walls of Vietnam's prisons lived tens of thousands more potential enemies of the regime, people like Tinh who valued their freedom and whose aim was to follow in the wake of the boat people.

What dangers the voyage might entail Tinh could only imagine from what he had heard. Le Mai tried to close her mind to them. The thought made her very afraid, but she and Tinh had shared so much in the seventeen years they had been together that where he went, she would go. And the children? They were pawns in a situation that was none of their doing and which yet had to be resolved. Tinh had not breathed a word to them about his intentions to escape; he hardly had the heart to involve them in an adventure in which they must surely suffer and might perhaps die. Had he the courage, had he even the right to do so? Night after night he lay awake, his mind tortured by a horrible vision. The frail wooden boat was being tossed here and there in a dark, mountainous sea. It capsized, and there was Le Mai clasping To and crying for help. Quang stretched out his arm, pleading to be saved, while Hue Hue, her pretty face convulsed, struggled helplessly. And where was Trung? Trung, who could not swim. He had disappeared. And it was for his sake more than anything else that Tinh had decided to escape. Was he right? The risk of dying at sea was perhaps greater for Trung than the risk of being killed in battle. But if Trung died, they all would die. If Trung survived the voyage, they all would.

With an effort Tinh would shake himself free of these dark thoughts, tiptoe to the children's rooms, Hue Hue in hers and the three boys in the room where they slept together. For some moments Tinh, in the half-light from the lamp outside, would stoop over the bed of each in turn, listening to their rhythmic breathing and watching the peace in their faces. What a moving contrast the sleeping children provided to the din and the violence of the world outside. Tinh would feel a wave of emotion, half love, half sorrow, as he thought to himself how unbearably innocent they were. With another effort his mind would clear, and back into it would come a single, lucid thought: "We must get out, all of us. We've always done things together. If we must die, then we will die together."

In March 1978 the Hanoi government announced that all trading and business operations of "bourgeois" elements were to be abolished. In Ho Chi Minh City some thirty thousand businesses were closed down and their stocks confiscated. The Chinese, who dominated the private business sector in South Vietnam, were the hardest hit, although Tinh, whose first business had been closed down long ago, had not much more to lose. It was the children who stood to suffer; it was common talk that the government intended to ban Chinese children from Vietnamese schools and prohibit the Chinese from having their own.

There remained too the ever-present threat of war between Vietnam and Kampuchea. At the end of 1977, after heavy fighting on the borders, Vietnamese troops had advanced on

48

the Kampuchean capital Phnom Penh, then withdrawn. Now, as April came, it brought more rumors in the press and from the grapevine, this time of war between Vietnam and Kampuchea's great ally, China; this could make things even more unpleasant for Chinese living in Vietnam. Though most of them had taken Vietnamese nationality, there was always the fear that in the event of war with China, Hanoi might whip up feeling against them as saboteurs, spies, and fifth-columnists—while taking care that their boys and girls of military age were called up. They were badly needed for the armed forces. Trung would certainly be called up, which would mean an almost certain sentence of death, for it was well known among the Chinese that their conscript sons were sent where the fighting was thickest—"just to get rid of them," it was said.

The situation in Vietnam was looking bleak, especially for the Chinese. Until now few of them had left Vietnam. Henceforth tens of thousands in the North were to flee to China; tens of thousands more in the South took to the sea. Tinh himself hesitated not a moment longer. Escape they must, the whole family, and the sooner the better. The risks had to be faced.

By now Tinh had saved and buried enough gold, which was just as well, for in May the government dealt another blow to the South. A common currency for the whole country was introduced; it caused a catastrophic devaluation of the South's *dong* and struck indiscriminately at both rich and poor, Vietnamese and Chinese. The people of both communities now faced a common enemy, the government, whose empty promises of a share-out of wealth had not materialized.

There was no time to lose. At the end of May, Tinh, after a word to Le Mai about his intentions, went to see an old friend, Ba Dan, who lived nearby. Ba, who was about Tinh's age, had also been called up during the war and had served in the Vietnamese navy, in riverboats. He had never been to sea. Formerly a man of property, Uncle Ba, as the family called him, had seen all his fortune confiscated by the state since the Communist takeover. Tinh knew that Ba was planning to escape. He asked to join him. Ba told him that he had already made some calculations based on a score of families, about half of them from Cantho province, half from Saigon.

With an average of four to five people per family, that would make about ninety passengers. The price, Ba reckoned, would work out at 5 ounces troy of gold per head. Tinh would have to pay 30 ounces—just for his family and himself. He had the money, he told Ba. "It will take a day or two" he began. Ba nodded; he understood of course that Tinh would have to do a little digging.

Tinh knew he could trust Ba, but he was less sure of his friend's ability as a sailor. "Are you sure you can handle the boat?" he asked. "Don't worry," Uncle Ba reassured him. "The young man they call Chu Nhi will be coming with us. He's a motor mechanic and knows about boats; I shall simply do the organizing." That satisfied Tinh. Then Ba warned him, "Of the twenty or so heads of families I have contacted, mostly ruined businessmen like ourselves"—he laughed wryly—"no one knows who else is involved. That must go for you, Tinh. You will deal directly with me, and don't worry about any-one else. I'll let you know soon about the boat and how you can help."

A week later, Uncle Ba called at Tinh's. Le Mai was away at the market, the children had left for school. Tinh was alone except for Co Ut, a cousin of his who acted as housekeeper and nanny; she came in daily and could be trusted. After greeting Tinh, Ba said quietly, "I want you to come straight away to see the boat." The two men left the house and, making sure that they were not followed, walked away chatting nonchalantly along the narrow road that led down to the small river, the Cau Cui, less than a mile away. Near the river the road petered out into a vague track that led among the tall reeds and mangroves down to the shallow muddy inlets at the river's edge. A few minutes later, Ba stopped and pointed. "There she is," he said to Tinh. Some yards away Tinh saw a wooden boat half stuck in the mud. A slack rope curved down from its low prow and wound itself around a rotting tree.

Tinh knew nothing about the sea or about boats, but at the sight of this one his heart sank. She was a riverboat, that much Tinh could tell, about forty feet long with a lot of freeboard, and, a little abaft the beam, a small pilothouse squatting on the flat deck, which extended from stem to stern. She doesn't look much of a sea boat, Tinh thought, but he said nothing to Uncle Ba. He couldn't afford to object. Somehow they would have to reach Malaysia in this frail, flat, and inadequate riverboat.

Then he thought of the ninety passengers the boat was to carry. Again Tinh said nothing. It must work, he thought. We'll make it somehow. He asked Ba, "How about the engine?" "Come and take a look," replied Uncle Ba, and they pushed their way through the reeds and climbed aboard the boat by a short ladder. Tinh was a little more at home with engines, rude and clumsy though they were compared to the delicate mechanism of his timepieces. But no one, however expert, can judge the condition of a motor without hearing it run, and this was out of the question at the moment. All Tinh could say as he surveyed the four-cylinder diesel engine was, "Well, it looks all right." Ba again reassured him. "Don't worry; we'll leave all that to Chu Nhi. He knows all about engines, especially this one. He's okayed it. He's promised me it will get us to Malaysia in five days or so. The rendezvous, by the way, will be back at the marketplace. From there we'll use a couple of sampans to ferry the passengers the mile or so here, to the boat."

"Now, Tinh," Uncle Ba went on, "we've got to collect four hundred gallons of diesel and get it aboard the boat. I count on you to help with some of it. We need food, water, and medicines too—basic ones, antiseptics, aspirin, and so on. We'll have to give the babies and small children a sleeping pill to stop them crying while we get aboard and keep them quiet till we reach the open sea. From here we're two hundred yards from the big river, Hau Giang. We have to go another forty miles downstream on the Hau Giang to the sea, and we could be stopped by a patrol boat. That isn't the moment for the babies to wake up and start crying."

Tinh and the other heads of family set about the task of collecting the necessary stores. Food, mostly rice, and medicine were no problem, but with the diesel fuel the greatest caution was needed. A small quantity came from stocks saved from the normal ration; the greater part was bought on the black market, where everybody traded, including the officials, soldiers, and police. The only difference was that the latter traded indirectly, stealing fuel from government stocks and handing it over to a friend or relative to sell on the black market, where no questions were asked. Corruption, still as rampant as it had been under the Diem and Thieu regimes, had provoked the Communist party journal *Hoc Tap* to admit that "the *can bo* are bewitched and tempted by a materialistic side of life."

Tinh began to make his stockpile of diesel fuel, hiding the containers in any convenient place he could find—in cupboards, under floorboards, in the bathroom, under bushes in the garden. Hue Hue and her brothers knew that their father was hiding containers, but did not know what was in them.

Tinh's store of diesel was carried in small lots to the hidden boat. Only once did Tinh himself undertake the dangerous mission; it was Uncle Ba who, as organizer, accepted it as his responsibility. The containers of diesel were packed into a *xe loi*, a small trailer attached to a bicycle. On top of the containers were piled innocent-looking fruit and vegetables. Uncle Ba on his *xe loi* never took the little path that led directly to the riverside and a few yards from the boat. Instead, he pedaled to another spot, a good half mile away, and there loaded his contraband merchandise into a small sampan. A friend then rowed downstream and, after disappearing around a bend in the river, glided into the reeds where Uncle Ba's boat lay hidden.

Once the police stopped him for a routine check. By a stroke of luck, Ba was not carrying fuel or supplies that day, but the passengers' luggage—if you could call it luggage; for each person a plastic bag containing a scanty change of clothing. The policeman examined Ba's load and asked, "Where are you going with that lot?" Uncle Ba could not say, "To the market," for the sale of secondhand clothes was illegal. The best he could manage was to answer, "I'm going to the country," to which the policeman replied: "Well, just hand over everything and go back home." Ba's boat people heard no more about the chances of taking any luggage with them.

During the summer months, the secret preparations went ahead. Tinh never gave an inkling of what he was about. Le Mai knew, but asked no questions. The children too had a feeling that their father was up to something, but even among themselves they never spoke about it. They were well aware that there were children at school who acted as informers to the secret police. On the other hand, there had been a pleasant change in their Vietnamese friends who, after the Communist takeover, had at first held aloof from them and other Chinese; now they were as friendly as ever. Vietnamese or Chinese, it no longer mattered. All had but one aim, to escape to freedom.

The children walked every day to school to follow the same routine. The Vietnamese language had now almost entirely taken the place of Cantonese, though they kept their own language alive at home. The hours given to indocrination were as long as ever.

The two little boys, Quang and To, still could not take Uncle Ho seriously. In secret they and their friends laughed, making up rhymes and jokes about him. With Trung it was another matter. Now sixteen, when boys begin to wonder at the meaning of life and dream up great plans for the future, Trung, once such a keen and promising boy, was unsettled and often moody and depressed.

He had heard the rumors of war and they frightened him. In the depths of his young being he felt he had much to give to life, yet it looked likely to him that his own life, hardly yet begun, would soon end, snuffed out by fire from the guns of boys like him, Kampuchean or Chinese. What was the use of killing each other for the sake of an ideology forced upon them willy-nilly by their rulers? Trung was in revolt. He felt lost and longed to escape from this dark, depressing hell. No one in Vietnam, he was sure, could want more than he to escape.

Sometimes he would talk things over with his sister. Young as she was, she always understood. Trung found that Hue Hue shared his longing to escape, though she was not unhappy at school in the same way that he was. She was bored; bored by the parrotlike political lectures, by sweeping the streets and weeding the public gardens. Hue Hue's young heart, like her brother's, was on fire. She dreamed of creative and exciting things, like traveling and exploring the culture and history of other lands but the new culture seemed to stifle all dreams. So Hue Hue, extrovert and dynamic, spent most of her energy on sports, running for the school athletics team, soon to compete at Hanoi, and winning table-tennis tournaments. She never missed the morning bike ride with her friends and her father— when he came, which now was more seldom. He seemed to be preoccupied with other things.

By now it was forbidden for anyone to travel beyond the district boundary. One day, however, Hue Hue and her friend Linh rode to a village twenty miles away to play in a table-tennis tournament. They did not set off for home until evening, and when they had still not arrived by nightfall, Tinh grew worried. Well after curfew had fallen, Hue Hue knocked on the door of her home. Tinh, his anxiety turned to anger, gave his daughter a good spanking. Hue Hue cried—not because the spanking hurt, but because her father, whom she worshiped, had suddenly turned into an enemy. Next day he said to her: "I'm sorry about last night. My nerves are rather on edge and I was very worried about you." Hue Hue kissed him, and that ended the matter; yet she wondered why his nerves were on edge. He must be worried about something. It must be escape. Instinctively, she put the thought from her mind. That was her father's business, not hers. Another thought then came to her: she went and knelt at the family shrine in the sitting room and prayed. "Whatever is worrying him, please, God, help my father."

Deeply religious, Hue Hue was sure Buddha could help. She did things for him, in his name, and naturally expected something—luck, success—in return. More seriously, she believed in his protection and in the protection of her ancestors. For who could tell the future? Hue Hue dreaded loneliness, being separated from her family. She put in a little prayer for herself. To "Help my father," she added, after a moment's thought: "And protect me. Keep me safe, whatever may happen to me."

Hue Hue had her parents to thank for her steady faith. In pre-Communist days, the children had all learned the first teachings of Buddhism, but it was to Hue Hue, when she was ten, that her parents had assigned the care of the four household shrines. While the temples of the fiercely anti-Communist Cao Dai and Hoa Hao sects (as well as the Christian churches) remained closed, the family could still worship at the temple of their sect, the Phat Giao. The police, however, kept a close watch in case of demonstrations by the worshipers and also checked that their offerings remained meager. The faithful felt frustrated.

More and more, the family made their devotions at the family shrines where they could worship privately without the police breathing down their necks. Outside the house stood an altar before which praise was given to the universe, the sun and moon, the clouds and rain and all the elements. Inside, in a corner of the living room, was the main altar for the worship of ancestors. It was made of wood and painted red and gold with a small gilt figure of the seated Buddha. In the same room, against the wall, was another, smaller altar for the saints and heroes of Chinese history; and on the floor, a fourth altar, where Hue Hue now prayed for the protection of the home and the family.

Every night Hue Hue made the round of the household shrines, placing joss sticks and lighting them; then on her knees, bent low, she would murmur a short prayer. She alone did this, on behalf of the family—and she believed in what she was doing.

To all outward appearances Hue Hue possessed an exceptionally happy and easygoing nature. She liked to laugh and have fun, to compete, too, with her many friends. Yet there was another side to her that was less obvious. She herself was only just becoming aware of it, of a force within her, steely, stubborn, and unyielding.

6

One day at the end of August, when the evening meal was finished and Co Ut, the housekeeper, had gone home, Tinh got up and quietly closed all the windows of the living room. The children wondered why, until he spoke to them in his calm voice: "Gather around, I have something to tell you." They came to him, and his voice became grave as he went on. "Listen. In about two weeks we are all going to escape, to leave our home forever and sail to Malaysia. From there I'll contact our cousin Ly To in Australia, which will be our new home. All the plans for the journey to Malaysia are made. There will be ninety people in the boat and we will leave at midnight on September twelfth, two nights before the full moon. By then the moon festival will have begun, so the curfew will be relaxed and we'll be able to move around with less danger from the police."

As Tinh talked, Le Mai looked absently in front of her. She had known his plans for weeks and did not want to listen; she was thinking how hard it would be to leave behind her own and Tinh's widowed mothers and her sister Phuong. The children, however, listened intently as Tinh continued: "You all know that the secret police have an eye on us. They have not bothered us seriously since they closed down the shop, but you must always remember that they or their informers may be watching and listening. They are the first danger to get by, though there will be others once we are at sea. The police, if they catch us, will put us in prison and then we'll be moved to a New Economic Zone. You little ones must not repeat a single word of what I have told you, even among yourselves. You go on as if you knew nothing."

The children's hearts beat faster as their father spoke. His voice, so calm and serious, made the danger feel more real. When he had finished speaking the children were silent. They needed time for his words to sink in, to work on their minds. They reacted in their own fashion. Hue Hue's one terror was that the police might catch them; she did not give a thought for the voyage, except that she longed for it to start. She could not help feeling sad at the idea of leaving, nor could she bring herself to believe that she would never again see her friends or their house, with all its memories. It hurt to think that she must leave her friends without even saying good-bye.

Trung, like his mother, said little; his thoughts too were far away. He was thrilled at the promise of a new life in Australia. Forget the police, he thought to himself; and the voyage too. In a few months we will be there. As for Quang and To, they were chattering excitedly about the police; they dreaded them, but it would be exciting to give them the slip and then sail away across the sea to Malaysia. "Bet you'll be the first to be. seasick," To laughed at Quang. "If you win I'll give you ten *dong*. They won't be any good anyway where we're going."

For the children the next two weeks seemed endless. In class their thoughts would often wander to the secret their father had told them. The teacher would snap, "Pay attention, there, what do you think you're dreaming of?" At the beginning of the second week in September, the family gathered at midday in a nearby restaurant for a farewell party. There were those who were leaving—Tinh and Le Mai and the children; Le Mai's younger sister, the children's twenty-three-year-old Aunt Binh; and their cousin Ly Tu Dan of about the same age. And there were those who were being left—Le Mai's mother, her other sister, Phuong, and her brother and his wife, as well as Tinh's mother, his sister Ngan, and his two brothers. Phuong had chosen the expensive menu: *cha gia* (spring rolls), *mi* (noodle soup), *nem nuong (brochette of beef)*, *bun tom* (grilled prawns and noodles), and *chao gao* (chicken and sticky rice)—all favorite dishes, which helped make the occasion seem festive. Yet not for an instant could any of them forget that this was the last time they would all be together.

The meal over, they walked to the home of Le Mai's mother for the final farewell. Tinh spoke the last words to those remaining behind. "This is the last time that we will see one another. Within a week you will get word that we have left. We ourselves will send word from Malaysia. Pray for us; we shall always pray for you." As they embraced for the last time, they were all in tears.

When at last September 12 arrived, the children were packed off to school as usual. If the housekeeper felt that their good-byes were unusually affectionate, her placid face betrayed no surprise. As the last class of the afternoon broke up, Hue Hue felt that she could not deceive her friends to the point of saying the usual, "Good-bye, see you tomorrow." She waved and called out "Good-bye," hardly able to believe that it was forever.

A little before then, a man had brought word to Tinh from Uncle Ba that he was to leave the house at 6 P.M. sharp and go to warn another family in his neighborhood to rendezvous forthwith at the marketplace, Ninh Kieu, beside the small river Cau Cui. Tinh's own family were to gather at the same spot. The departure was on.

At midday, as the housekeeper made ready to return to her home, Le Mai stoped her and Tinh said, "We are going to leave very soon. Don't come back, we shall say good-bye to you now." As she had done earlier that morning with the children, the housekeeper showed no surprise. They talked for some minutes, and then as they took leave, Tinh said: "Come back after we have left and help yourself to anything you want from the house. But not before five days after you hear we have gone." Five days. By then the family should be in Malaysia.

The children were all home by 4 P.M. Le Mai gave them rice and sweet pork, telling them: "Eat all you can. We'll be going hungry for the next week." When they had eaten she said to them, "Now go quietly to your rooms and change." Each of the children and their parents had set aside some old, worn clothes in which they could pass as fisherfolk. Hue Hue slipped out of her clean school uniform and changed into a grubby striped blouse and a flowery-pattern pajama, over which she pulled an old pair of black cotton trousers. She had also kept a checked jacket, threadbare at the elbows, to wear during the cool nights at sea. On her feet she wore leather sandals with a strap over the toes. Le Mai's outfit was similar. The boys had taken off their clean white shirts and carefully creased blue shorts and thrown them on the bed. Giggling, they pulled on the disguises that Tinh had procured for them and himself, the salt-stained nondescript shirt, black trousers, and typical fisherman's sandals.

Warned by Uncle Ba's unfortunate encounter earlier with the police, the family took nothing with them. The police

61

knew too well that people carrying luggage were people bent on escaping. But each member of the family now discreetly concealed a quantity of U.S. dollar bills that Tinh had obtained on the black market; the money might come in handy for bribing the police. Tinh himself had hidden fifteen ounces troy of gold and five hundred-dollar bills in a belt around his waist. Le Mai, Aunt Binh, cousin Dan, and the three boys each had two hundred dollar-bills hidden in their clothing. To Hue Hue, Tinh had entrusted, besides two hundred-dollar bills, a solid gold necklace, which she wore beneath the buttoned-up collar of her blouse.

Like a good clockmaker, Tinh had synchronized all the timepieces in his house to the correct hour, which was now 5:45 P.M. He called Le Mai and the children to him and motioned them to follow him to the family shrine. There, for some minutes, they worshiped, bowing their heads to the ground before a small image of the Buddha and praying: "Lord Buddha, take care of all those we are leaving behind. And protect us one and all and lead us in safety to Malaysia and freedom." Then they stood up and Tinh said: "It's almost six o'clock. You each know exactly what do to. I'm leaving now to warn our neighbors, then I will go straight on to the market-place and we'll find each other there. Keep just close enough to remain in sight; act natural, but be careful. We'll leave the door open and cousin Co Ut will be there, so that if the police call she will tell them we've gone out for the evening. If anything goes wrong, come straight back to the house and stay inside." With that he was gone.

It was Hue Hue's turn to leave next. Before she did so, she ran back to her bedroom. Standing in the doorway, she glanced around, fixing in her mind the pale blue walls covered with photos of her family and friends and of her favorite actress

Chan Chan. On the shelf above her bed were stacked her table-tennis paddles and on the bed itself, tidily folded, her neat school uniform, white shirt and blue pleated skirt, with a heap of schoolbooks. On the pillow reclined her doll, wearing the new shirt and blue jeans she had just made for it. Good-bye, all of you and everything, she thought, and had to force back the tears. Then, firmly, thirteen-year-old Hue Hue shut the door behind her, closed it on her life in Vietnam. The odor of sweet pork and rice hanging about the house made her think: No more good things like that for a while.

A fond pat but no tears for the dog, Dolly, and Hue Hue was standing by the open front door with her mother and brothers. "See you all at the marketplace," she said. "Be careful." She turned and began walking toward Ninh Kieu, the marketplace, a half-mile away. A few minutes after her came Trung, then Quang, each taking a slightly different route. Finally Le Mai left with her youngest boy, To, and her sister Binh. As arranged, Le Mai had left the front door unlocked.

Hue Hue and her family, with the rest of the ninety people intent on escaping that night, were but a few of the hundreds converging on the Ninh Kieu for the moon-festival celebrations. Hue Hue walked at a leisurely pace, yet every fiber of her small body was taut. This was another game, an escaping game, which, like running or table tennis, would need all her wits and determination if she was to win it. She noticed with some perplexity that her sandals seemed unusually heavy. Every now and again they slipped off her feet. She did not discover till later that Tinh had inserted five *la*—gold leaves— between the upper and lower soles, which added two ounces to the weight of each sandal.

At about half-past six Hue Hue reached the market. Dusk

was falling; the night was warm and not a breath of wind stirred the palm trees. Stars were beginning to shine in a cloudless, darkening sky; festive music played throughout the marketplace. That night was one of the most beautiful that Hue Hue could remember. She loitered for a while near the food shops that, with the bus company's ticket office, were the only establishments open. She noticed a few policemen strolling among the crowds but did not feel afraid of them. The moon festival was a festival for children, and so there were many of them in the marketplace, each with a lantern, each eating candy and moon-cake that made Hue Hue's mouth water, while their parents greeted their friends, chatted, and laughed. The moon festival seemed to have put everybody back into a good mood.

Scanning the crowds for the rest of the family, Hue Hue had no difficulty in spotting them in the glare of the gaslights; each made a sign of mutual recognition; then, still keeping their distance, they moved toward the bank of the Cau Cui. Hue Hue sat down on the ground at the riverbank, and began to chat with her brother Trung, her young Aunt Binh, and her cousin Dan.

About twenty paces away, she could just make out her father and mother seated on a bench with Quang and To. They too were chatting quietly. Tinh had just remarked to Le Mai: "It is hard to believe that fifteen years ago, on this very spot, we opened a fine shop, and now we are refugees fleeing to save our lives." Hue Hue's thoughts were running on the same theme.

On the river, boats and sampans kept coming and going, ferrying people and vehicles to and fro from one end of National Route 4 to where it began again on the opposite bank. Close to where Hue Hue and the others were sitting, two sampans floated at their moorings. Those two weather-beaten little craft had a vital role to play. Everyone had been warned that when they saw two men walk down to the sampans and climb aboard, it was the signal for the passengers to embark.

The evening darkened into night. In the marketplace the crowd jostled and laughed, music played, and children danced, lanterns in hand. The festival was in full swing.

It was around eight o'clock when Hue Hue noticed two men walking casually down to where the sampans were moored only a few yards away from her. She nudged Trung. "Look," she whispered, "the signal!" A moment later, out of the crowd, Uncle Ba appeared at her side. He bent down and in a quiet voice said, "Come along, Hue Hue and Trung and the rest of you; all aboard!" Others followed, some carrying children, some leading them by hand, walking toward the sampans.

Soon Hue Hue's sampan, crammed with people including Uncle Ba, put off into the river and headed downstream; its gunwales were almost level with the water, which came seeping over at the slightest rolling movement. Hue Hue was sure the sampan was going to sink, but five minutes later it was bumping along the side of the big boat and Hue Hue, Trung, Binh, and Dan, and all the others were climbing aboard up a short wooden ladder. Hue Hue sat down on deck, Trung next to her. She looked around at the faces, dimly visible in the moonlight, to make sure that her parents and brothers were there, and discovered that they were not. She remarked on this to Trung, who reassured her: "Don't worry, Hue Hue, they will be along with the next lot."

Minutes went by. The second sampan, followed some moments later by Uncle Ba's with another load of passengers, came alongside. Carefully, Hue Hue searched the face of every passenger, until the last one stepped on deck. Still no sign of her parents and brothers. By now, she was so worried that she called out to Uncle Ba, who just then was climbing back down the ladder into his sampan. "Where are my parents and my brothers?" she asked, almost crying. Uncle Ba called back, "Don't worry, Hue Hue, I'll bring them along with the next lot." Then he and his sampan disappeared upstream into the darkness.

As he pulled in toward the riverbank at the marketplace, something looked amiss to Uncle Ba. The sampan drifted closer to the riverbank. Then, to his consternation, he saw that one of the waiting passengers was being questioned by a policeman, automatic rifle in hand. He saw Tinh standing a pace away from them. Ba stepped ashore and from a safe distance waited to see what would happen.

Tinh, meanwhile, despite the gold and dollar bills he carried on him, decided that this was not the moment to try bribing the police. His courage deserting at the thought that he, too, might be questioned and searched, he began to tremble visibly. Le Mai did the same, while the two little boys just stood there, petrified. They heard the policeman ask the man, "What are you all doing, hanging around here?" and the man's unhurried answer, "We are waiting to buy bus tickets to return to our homes in the country." The policeman appeared satisfied and walked away. As he did so, Tinh and his family and all the other fugitives, the forty of them who remained ashore, made haste to disperse, disappearing under the palm trees, fading into the shadows. For them the riverbank at Ninh Kieu had become a decidedly unhealthy place.

As Tinh hurried away, half-running with his family, he passed within a few feet of his friend Ba. With so many people about, Ba could only speak in a loud whisper. "Come on, Tinh," he urged. "If you are coming, come now or it will be too late. I'm leaving." Ba was about to add, "Hue Hue and Trung are already aboard," when Tinh cut him short. "How can I possibly come with you," he pleaded, "and leave my two older children behind?" Without giving Ba a chance to explain, he rushed off into the dark with Le Mai and the two little boys.

Uncle Ba turned back toward his sampan. It was no longer there. He made for one of the waiting ferry-sampans, climbed into it, and pressed forty *dong*, instead of the usual two, into the hand of the astonished boatman. "Take it and keep your mouth shut," he ordered. "Row me downstream until I tell you to stop." Five minutes later the confused and frightened Uncle Ba was aboard the boat. To a young man who sat counting the passengers as they boarded Ba hissed, "How many?" "Fifty including you," the man replied. "All right. Pass the word around that we're leaving this instant. The police have discovered us." As he spoke, Ba fumbled with the engine controls, found the starter button, and pushed it. The diesel motor spluttered into life, then settled down, turning over steadily. "Cast off," ordered Ba, and called for Chu Nhi. "Chu Nhi, where are you? Come and take over!" But Chu Nhi, who knew all about motors, especially this one, and was able to steer a compass course, was still on dry land, his pocket compass in his shirt pocket. Chu Nhi had missed the boat and there was not a soul on board competent to sail it.

7

In the wheelhouse Uncle Ba, his nerves taut, peered forward until his nose nearly touched the glass window. Next to him stood Trung, who Ba had told to stand by as messenger and lookout. Easing the boat away from its hidden moorings, Ba headed her carefully down the Cau Cui and into the broad waters of the Hau Giang, the river that led down to the sea. From his brief war service in navy riverboats, Ba knew he could get the boat that far—he did not allow his thoughts to wander further. He must concentrate, get safely through the river traffic, keep a sharp lookout for the river police. He could see no reason why a riverboat with most of its fifty passengers hidden below deck should attract attention. All the same he warned Trung, "Keep your eyes skinned."

Soon Ba began to relax a little and it was then that he became conscious of a commotion below deck, sounds of wailing and moaning. "Go and see what's the matter," Ba told Trung, who disappeared. A few minutes later he was back. "It's the families who've been split up. They're going nearly mad. There's a girl of twelve who's crying and crying because her parents have been left behind. Other people are calling for their wives or their husbands and children." Ba said nothing, but continued through the glass of the wheelhouse. He was aware of a disturbing feeling that the boat, from the moment she got under way, was to be an unhappy one.

Trung had been able to have a few words with Hue Hue. Neither of them yet quite realized the drama of their situation. They had often talked about escaping alone. Well, this was it. They were completely on their own, cut off from their family. Trung said, "Get some sleep, Hue Hue," and went to join Ba in the wheelhouse. Below, on one of the wooden planks that had been laid on the cross-members of the boat, Hue Hue dozed, wedged tightly between two other people and maddeningly aware that she was being devoured by mosquitoes. Then she fell asleep, slumped against one of her neighbors. Occasionally she awoke and shifted herself from one uncomfortable position to another. Through a tiny porthole she saw palm trees go by and knew that the boat was still sailing down the river.

Tinh had shepherded his family safely through the dark back to the house. He opened the door and his cousin Co Ut, astonished, asked, "Why have you come back?" "The police," replied Tinh, quickly adding, "and Trung and Hue Hue. They're not back?" "Not yet," said Co Ut, "but they must be on their way." Tinh, Le Mai, and the boys, still feeling frightened, went to the sitting room. A few minutes later they heard the door open. "Must be them." But the two people at the door were friends of Tinh, and during the next twenty minutes more friends arrived. All were members of the escape group who lived near the police station and dared not go home. Tinh and Le Mai welcomed them mechanically, asking each one, "Have you seen Trung and Hue?" No one had seen either of the two children.

Tinh's clocks were all striking midnight; their concerted chimes nearly drove him mad, for they told him that three hours had passed since he last saw Ba, and that Trung and Hue Hue were still missing. Where could they be? Arrested? If so, he would find out tomorrow. Still at the moon festival? Tinh dismissed the idea. Those two loved to have fun, but they would never have disobeyed his instruction to return home should anything go wrong. Then he remembered the words that Ba had called after him: "Come on, Tinh, I'm leaving." Were his children with Ba? He spoke to Le Mai: "I think they must have left with Uncle Ba and the rest. Perhaps he'll turn back, then we can join them tomorrow." But Le Mai was not to be consoled by such a frail hope. She had been on the verge of breaking down since they returned to the house, and now through her tears she reproached Tinh. "You should never have allowed the children to get into such terrible danger." Tinh, venturing a last hope, replied, "But if they are with Ba, they should be safe enough."

When Tinh, exhausted, finally stretched out on his bed, it was nearly 3 A.M., six hours since the boat had left. He was now sure that Hue Hue and Trung were in it. Alone with his thoughts in the dark, his optimism vanished. When, if ever, would he see them again? He turned over and cried quietly to himself. In their beds Le Mai and the two little boys were crying too. No one slept that night.

Next morning Tinh's uninvited guests left his house and slipped back to their own, but others came to call on him. Tinh was well known in Cantho. "We saw you down at the river last night," they said, eager for gossip. "Were you trying to escape?" Tinh, putting on a brave face, replied as politely as he could: "How could I have been trying to escape since I'm still here?" All the same, the gossip spread. It was bound,

70

sooner or later, to reach the ears of the police. Meanwhile, Tinh and Le Mai forced themselves to carry on as if it were just another day. Quang and To were sent off to school, but not before Tinh told them: "If you are asked about your brother and sister, say that they have gone to Saigon."

Half a dozen boys and girls, friends of Trung and Hue Hue, came to the house that evening. They—and others, no doubt, including the teachers—had noticed their absence in class; that must mean that they had escaped. Tinh led them inside to Le Mai and the boys. One of Hue Hue's friends, Hoa, spoke for the rest. "We want to say how sorry we are and how much we all miss them. We shall go to the temple and pray that they will return safely to you." But not all the sympathy of their own and the children's friends could alter the cruel reality of the two empty places at table. As Le Mai later said: "We ate rice mixed with tears."

Three nights after the children's disappearance, Tinh, sleeping fitfully, had a strange dream. He saw Trung and Hue Hue on a rock in the middle of the sea. They were both naked and were clearly alive. Then, bending over him, Tinh saw an aged saffron-robed priest, with drooping mustaches and a long white beard. "How many children have you?" asked the bonze, and Tinh replied, "Four, but two are away." "Yes," said the old man, "two are away and they are both dead." Tinh struggled to free himself from the dream. He sat up, sweating. "No," he said aloud, "I saw them, they are both still alive." Straight away he got up, crept silently to the family shrine, and prayed. "Keep them safe, let them live. Send them back to us."

8

The motion of the boat awoke Hue Hue. She opened her eyes and realized that they were well out to sea. Trung was squatting next to her. Somehow he had managed to fit himself in between her and the next passenger. Drowsily she said, "Hullo, Chung Co. Have you seen the others?" But before Trung could reply, Hue Hue had realized "the others" were not there. She burst into tears and her brother, weary after a night on watch, felt himself being carried away by his sister's crying. He, too, began to cry and they sat there, wedged one against the other in the crowd, utterly lost. After a while Trung took hold of himself. "Cheer up, Hue Hue," he said. "We'll stick together, whatever happens."

Hue Hue's eyes were fixed on the small porthole. At one moment it was filled with pale blue sky; then, as the boat rolled, the horizon came up and erased the sky until there was only blue-gray sea. Down came the horizon again until the porthole was again full of sky. Hue Hue felt very seasick. "Come on, let's go up on deck," Trung said. They managed to squeeze side by side into the row of people sitting on deck back against the boat's side, their knees gathered into their clasped hands. Hue Hue remarked to Trung: "To think there should have been forty more on board! Already we are packed like sardines."

The sun was riding up into an empty blue sky, blazing hotter every minute. Hue Hue held up her checked jacket to protect herself, but her arms soon tired and she lay down, covering her head with it. All but a few of the passengers were seasick like her. The retching and vomiting, the mess, the stench mixed with diesel fumes: Hue Hue realized that her own misery was caused not so much by the motion of the boat as by the stinking, stifling atmosphere. "Come with me, Trung," said Hue Hue, and began to make toward the bow, not walking—that was impossible—but crawling on all fours across the splayed, groaning bodies on deck. Once up in the bow, with a breeze blowing on her face, Hue Hue felt a little better. Trung too; for the first time since leaving, they exchanged a smile. It was only a fleeting one, however, for Hue Hue suddenly remembered: "This time yesterday," she said, on the verge of tears, "we were on our way to school with Quang and To."

At the other extremity of the boat, in the stern, were the heads, the latrines. There was sitting room for two on a plank placed athwartships, each end supported by a beam that extended on either side just beyond the stern, so that the excrement would drop straight into the sea—a precarious perch, but at least screened from the public gaze by two half-barrels sectioned vertically.

In spite of the breeze, Trung and Hue Hue's seasickness persisted. Yet they felt hungry. Hue Hue nibbled at a *cusan*, a sweet, pulpy fruit; she sucked it a little and handed it to Trung, who did the same. For days, this was to be their daily portion, for the nausea and the motion of the boat made their stomachs revolt at anything more substantial. Others, recovering from their seasickness, became ravenous for solid food. They quarreled and swore at each other as they fought for their share of the rice and dried fish. Drinking water was rationed to a cup a day. It was not enough to assuage their thirst, and many of the people found some relief by jumping into the sea, a rope around them, and being trailed for a few minutes alongside. Hue Hue enjoyed this, but the salt water, as it dried out, began to eat into her striped blouse and flowered pajamas. So she remained aboard, parched from thirst, watching the waves roll past the boat and sending an occasional shower of spray over her.

When Uncle Ba was not steering, he tried to put some order into life on board, rationing the food and organizing the passengers into groups of about ten, each with a leader, and telling them to take special care of the aged and the mothers and children. Hue Hue's group included Trung, cousin Dan, and Aunt Binh. Binh was sick and depressed, and Hue Hue, too, felt so helpless with seasickness that she almost wanted to die. But Van, a girl in her twenties who was a friend of the family, urged her to hold on; it would be for only a few more days. Hue Hue was lucky with her group. Elsewhere the system broke down and it was everyone for himself.

Uncle Ba, as uncertain of his authority over the ship's company as of the direction in which it was heading, bravely tried to keep up his own and everybody else's spirits. "Don't worry," he reassured them, "last night I was navigating by the stars. We are on a steady course to Malaysia. A few more days and we shall be there." But on reaching the mouth of the River Hau Giang that morning, poor Uncle Ba had also reached the limit of his navigational experience. He had never been to sea and, on meeting it at the river's mouth, was at a complete loss. He should have altered course some 90° to the west. That would have put the boat on a course to the Malaysian coast, with a landfall somewhere near Pulau Bidong, the island refugee camp that had opened two months earlier, in July. Instead he swung the helm some 30° eastward and kept straight on into the middle of the most dangerous waters in Southeast Asia—the South China Sea.

The first day out, the boat began to take water, which the bilge pump spewed back into the sea. Next morning, the engine faltered, picked up, faltered again, and stopped. In a calm sea the boat hove to, and Hue Hue watched as a small group of people bent over the engine. As they tinkered with it, she heard them repeating *zoupape, zoupape*. She had never heard the word but it intrigued her and she asked Trung what it meant. He told her. "We borrowed it from the French, *soupape*, valve." The engine had valve trouble, a serious defect at any time but a dangerous one on the high sea, especially in a leaky boat. When the engine stopped working, the bilge pump stopped working too. The boat began to take water fast, and in the cramped space below deck men began frantically bailing, their plastic buckets full of water being passed back along a line formed by other passengers to be tipped into the sea and passed back again to the front of the line. An hour went by, then another, as the powerless boat drifted. During that time two merchantmen passed not more than a half mile away and the people on the roof of the wheelhouse waved energetically. Their efforts were in vain; without a sign of recognition, the big ships sailed on their way, while the boat people hurled insults and curses after them, not believing that their signals could be so flagrantly ignored. Nothing that had happened so far had so demoralized them. They felt better when they heard the engine splutter once more into life; a thin cheer went up, and the boat was again under way, making about three miles an hour.

The second day out from land was ending; by now, the

passengers, though they did not realize it, had almost crossed the main shipping lanes and were heading for an empty desert of water. Since the engine failure they had passed one more merchantman, but Ba had warned: "Don't make any sign. It looks like a Soviet ship." The Russians were known to pick up boat people and land them back in Vietnam, a fate worse than drowning.

That night the engine stopped twice more, and each time pandemonium broke out below, with the fetid air full of cries and swearwords—"Fix the engine, for God's sake; we're going to sink"—and the screaming of frightened children. Flashlights shone and buckets were again passed from hand to hand. A gale began blowing up—it was the tail of the monsoon season—and the helpless, overloaded boat, tossed here and there by the waves, took so much water that it felt as if it were going to capsize. Then the motor started up, the boat moved forward again, and the panic subsided.

All next day the gale blew and torrents of rain, cold and stinging, blotted out the horizon. The engine kept breaking down; each time it did so, the boat people bailed for their lives. On deck, the people at the end of the line, lashed by the rain, cold, drenched, and exhausted, began to protest. In vain Ba encouraged them: "Come on, stick to it, keep bailing or we're lost." They answered: "Nothing doing. The boat's going to sink anyway!" Others took their place. For another day and night the boat people fought the storms and the faulty engine and somehow kept their craft afloat.

At last the big seas subsided into long, heaving swells and flying fish scudded across the rolling purple-blue valleys of water. No spray flew and the sea no longer came pouring over the gunwales. A fiery sun sailed again into the sky and dried out the deck till it was warm. But the problem of the engine remained; bailing had become a routine operation. On the eighth day of the voyage, the sea became still and flat; not a breath of wind rippled its glassy surface. The engine seemed to catch the mood; though it still ran unevenly, sending vibrations through the length of the boat, it miraculously kept going. By evening huge, bulbing cumulus clouds had ballooned up high into the sky, reflecting and diffusing the last rays of the setting sun and forming an unbroken barrage whose lower surface almost touched the horizon. In the fading, pink-gold light the boat chugged on, throwing up a little phosphorescent bow wave that slid down each side until its dancing sparks were extinguished in the turbulence of the wake.

With Trung beside her, Hue Hue had been watching the sunset. Her thoughts temporarily distracted by its splendor, she forgot her pangs of hunger and the nausea that had cloyed her throat and the pit of her stomach for over a week. Life had dragged on painfully through long, anxious days and restless nights—days and nights punctuated by periods of stifling heat; by raging storms and the anguished cries of frightened people; by the frequent failures of an old and unreliable engine, whose pungent fumes mingled with the stench of sick humanity; and, at last, by the calm that had fallen over the sea and the boat itself.

Throughout the turmoil of the voyage, Hue Hue's thoughts had dwelt ceaselessly on her parents and brothers back in Vietnam. She was only thirteen; she missed her family terribly and cried whenever she imagined them at home. But Binh and Van had been sweet to her; Trung was always at her side; and Dan helped to encourage her.

She looked around the crowded deck. Where were they going, all these people, most of them unknown to her? Before them lay nothing but sea, stretching out to the horizon, and the clouds, now darkening into gray against a vivid blue-green sky.

It began to get chilly, so Hue Hue and Trung moved below, squeezed themselves in between some others, and sat down with their backs against the ship's side. As the day died so did the sound of garrulous voices. People were chatting quietly now, and peace and order had returned to the boat. Hue Hue and Trung began to doze.

Suddenly a harsh, grating sound and the crash of splitting timber jolted everyone into wakefulness. The boat came to an abrupt standstill. Through the broken hull water gushed past their feet and people shouted: "We're aground—everybody up on deck!" From their cramped quarters below, there followed a rush of old men and women, of mothers clasping their children to them or dragging them by the hand. The young men and girls clambered up last. Everyone on deck was talking excitedly. "We have hit land all right, but where? Malaysia? Thailand?" No one could answer, least of all Uncle Ba. Then above the hubbub came a voice, and a young man pointed into the fading light: "Look, a ship! There! A ship at anchor!" People peered after him and cried: "Yes, it's a ship! We're saved!" Some shook hands and embraced; others were too weary for joy.

Few of them slept that night, partly through excitement, partly because they had to camp as best they could on deck. The boat was filling fast, until, around midnight, the water, a yard deep inside the hull, had risen to the level of the sea outside. At least that would keep the boat on an even keel.

To Hue Hue the boat now felt as solid as a house. Her sickness disappeared, but like everybody else, she could not sleep. She lay there on the hard deck in the dark, her cardigan over her, a frightened little girl marooned somewhere in the middle of the sea.

9

The sympathy of friends helped to galvanize Tinh out of his grief. He must do something, but great caution was needed, otherwise he risked getting into worse trouble. Tinh considered the situation. Every householder in Vietnam had to declare to the local authorities the particulars of each person living under his roof. Naturally, Tinh had declared Le Mai and his four children. The law also required that any change should be reported within a week. Tinh thought, "No. Let the police find out for themselves." That would give him more time to make inquiries.

Tinh's best hope was through the grapevine that linked those who had already left the country to those who had stayed behind. He wrote a letter to his cousin Ly To in Sydney and another to a refugee friend in Manila. To yet another friend, about to embark secretly for Malaysia, Tinh asked for news of his children should the friend find any there on arrival. It would of course take some time before Tinh could hope to get any response to these inquiries. Meanwhile he tried another line. He had heard that a boat had been intercepted by a naval patrol in the last few days and the people aboard taken to Con Son, Vietnam's Devil's Island. Con Son lay about 125 miles out to sea beyond the Mekong delta. One of Tinh's friends offered to go there and find out from the prison officials if they held two children by the name of Tran Dieu Trung and Tran Hue Hue. He was back two days later with the news that the two children were not on the island.

Dawn revealed to Hue Hue and Trung that they were indeed on an island—but where, not one of the boat people had the remotest idea. Even a qualified navigator might have been perplexed, for it was a small island, indeed no more than a coral reef. In 1829 Captain Ladd, master of the East Indiaman *Austin*, had noted the reef in his journal as "lying even with the water's edge several leagues to the SW of West London Reef." Fourteen years later, Captain Spratly of the whaler *Cyrus* reported that "having lowered without success after Sperm Whales, they going fast to the ENE among the reefs," the following day "an extensive reef was seen from the mast-head extending in a SSE and NNW direction, about four miles. . . . It is level with the water's edge, with large black rocks visible about the middle and though the water was very smooth, broke heavily from one end to the other of it." Captain Spratly reported that next day "a low sandy island was discovered—inhabited by thousands of the feathered tribe." Of these two "dangers" he concluded: "One I call Ladd's Reef, after Captain Ladd—who appears first to have seen it; the other Spratly's Sandy Island." The *China Sea Pilot* describes Ladd Reef (as it is now called) as a reef composed of coral enclosing a lagoon with a bottom of white sand that dries in parts.

Before the boat people ran onto Ladd Reef a number of other craft had grounded there, among them a submarine. But by 1978 it and earlier wrecks had all been torn asunder and, except for their solid parts like engines and boilers, had been swept away by the ceaseless attrition of the sea. Only three wrecks are today marked on British Admiralty chart 2660 B: an unidentified vessel at the northeast corner of the reef; a large cargo steamer, the *Tuscany*, at the northwest; and, at the southern end, a motor fishing vessel, the *Chung Yang No. 1*.

The *Tuscany*, 7,207 gross tons, owned by the Peggy Navigation Company and sailing under the Liberian flag, had run aground in December 1962 while on a voyage from Hong Kong to North Borneo. The crew of forty-one had been rescued by the Royal Australian Navy frigate *Quiberon* and the salvage tug *Salvonia*.

The *Chung Yang No. 1*, 290 gross tons, owned by the Dae Jim Shipping Company of Korea, sailed on August 9, 1974, from the Java fishing grounds for Pusan, Korea, with a cargo of 130 tons of frozen tuna fish. Six days later it stranded after dark in heavy weather. Next morning its distress signals were seen by a passing vessel, which was unable to close in the shallow water. That evening an oil tanker made another unsuccessful attempt, and it was not until next day that the crew of twenty-six was taken off in the lifeboat of a third ship, the motor vessel *May Prince*.

In the case of each vessel, salvage operations were found to be too costly. So the *Tuscany* and the *Chung Yang No. 1* were left to rot and rust away on Ladd Reef.

The *China Sea Pilot* gives the position of the reef as 8°38′N, 111°40′E. It lies some 400 miles east of Con Son and a good 600 from the nearest point on the Malaysian coast, Uncle Ba's intended destination. His knowledge of celestial navigation had proved sadly wanting.

To the east, where the sun was rising, the ship sighted the evening before could now be seen clearly. Its hull and superstructure were white; it lay a half mile or so away and was apparently anchored. Ba called immediately for volunteers, and in a few minutes four men had stripped and climbed over the side of the boat. They waded waist deep some way, then began swimming. The other passengers watched, their eyes glued to the swimmers who had nearly disappeared from sight by the time they approached the ship half an hour later. Before they reached it, the watching people saw something that filled them with dismay. From the ship there arose, like a small white cloud, hundreds of seagulls. A groan went up. "The ship's deserted. It must be a wreck!" It was. Its name, *Chung Yang No. 1*, had become illegible during the four years it had been aground on Ladd Reef.

Two hours later the swimmers were back. It must have been about high tide, they said, when they reached the vessel. Its bow was just aground and the rest of the ship was in the water—which explained why, from a distance, it looked as if it were afloat. The men reported another wreck, much bigger— a merchantman with a black hull—which they had seen about two miles away on the other side of the reef. They had climbed aboard the smaller ship, the "white ship" as they called it, up a rope ladder hanging over the stern. (No doubt the last survivor from the *Chang Yang No. 1* four years previously had climbed down it into the *May Prince*'s lifeboat.) Obviously, the men said, the wreck would provide better shelter for everyone than their own half-sunk boat. There was firewood aboard, and rainwater had collected here and there on deck. On the reef itself there seemed to be plenty of shellfish. But it was going to be a tricky job getting everyone across to the wreck. The only hope would be to try at low tide.

Ba was in earnest discussion with Minh Hung, a Cantho businessman of fifty who, although he knew even less than Ba about how to sail the boat, had put down more money than anyone else for its purchase and was therefore the acknowledged chief. He and Ba agreed that everybody should stay with the boat for the time being while they investigated the possibility of refloating it. Ba had all available hands overboard in an attempt to push it off the reef, but the boat, full of several tons of water, refused to budge. Minh Hung then wanted to lighten it by removing the engine. But the problem of refloating the boat was not to be solved by two well-intentioned landlubbers; naval men, in the circumstances, would have written it off as a dead loss.

Nothing but rice, and not much of it, was left for the boat people to eat—and the sacks, stored below deck, were under water. When recovered, the rice had to be cooked in sea water over a fire kindled on deck with firewood that had somehow remained dry. Having eaten practically nothing for several days, Hue Hue was very thin, but she felt well and strong. Guided by Van, she now gladly undertook any job going, helping with the cooking, fetching and carrying for the mothers and the old people who were worn out and bewildered by the voyage and frightened by their present plight.

Two days after the grouding, a merchant ship, its hull painted white, passed so close that the details of its superstructure were visible. If only the boat people could have fired distress signals! But they had none. All they could do was wave desperately, with every light-colored thing they could lay hands on, jumping up and down and shouting hysterically. Heedless of their signals, the ship sailed on. As she watched it disappear, Hue Hue wept. The men aboard, she was sure, must have seen the boat people. That ship was the chance she and everyone else had prayed for, but it had vanished over the horizon.

Aunt Binh, Hue Hue noticed, was becoming more and more depressed. For some while now she had harped daily on the same theme. "Rather than suffer as we have done," she would say, "and end up by dying on this coral reef, we would have done better to stay in Vietnam." Then, for a long time, she would cry.

While Binh talked, Hue Hue remained silent, thinking. The incident of the passing ship had helped to focus things in her mind. On the one hand she felt a mood of resignation to what the future might hold, yet on the other a determination to resistance. It seemed to her that the experience she was living was a part of her destiny. Rightly or wrongly, the decision had been made to leave Vietnam; now it was up to her to follow her destiny. But in doing so, she was determined not to go down without a fight.

Two nights later, Hue Hue was sleeping—peacefully, for once—when she woke up suddenly. It was pitch dark and the boat seemed to be moving. Before she had time to sit up, cascades of water were crashing down on top on top of her. Feeling as if she were about to drown, she fought for breath; she heard people scream and vaguely saw them try to grab the side of the boat. It had been hit sideways by a huge wave that swept right over it. Torrents of water poured below and flooded the deck. Hue Hue and Trung staggered to the side of the boat and with everyone else clung there, waiting for another wave. Fortunately, it never came. That one great wave might well have been generated by a passing ship.

Not long after the wave struck, two voices could be heard in fierce altercation above the commotion. Minh Hung's wife was protesting to her husband that everyone should leave the ill-starred vessel and move to the wreck, the "white ship." "Our boat's got an evil spell on it!" she shrieked. Minh Hung disagreed, pursuing his old, pathetic argument. "We must first try taking out the engine, lightening the boat, and refloating it." The engine was already half out; the great wave had smashed the wooden bearers on which it was mounted. But that did not help.

When daylight came, more people joined in the discussion. An hour later, the debate ended, with a vote against moving on that particular day; according to the calendar it was a day of bad luck. A dozen young people, led by the four young men who had swum to the white ship, protested. "If we are going to die," one of them said "we'd rather die on the white ship than here." Binh, Van, and Dan agreed. Hue Hue had been listening intently. Her own mind was made up. To Trung she whispered: "We must go with them."

The difference between low and high tide was about 5 feet—not far short of Hue Hue's own height. Because some of the group, Trung included, could not swim, the young people—Hue Hue, Binh, and Van were the only girls among them—decided to wait for the tide to fall in the hope that the nonswimmers would not get out of their depth. Between their sunken boat and the wreck of the white ship there stretched a half mile or so of flat, calm sea that broke only here and there where patches of coral appeared above the surface.

It looked easy enough. When the time came, they slid overboard into the sea. They took nothing with them save some cooked rice and a cigarette lighter; these were placed in a plastic container that one of the youths carried above water. Hue Hue took off her sandals, tied them together with a piece of string, and slung them around her neck. Then she dropped into the sea. She was in her depth. Trung was about to follow when she stopped him. "Keep behind me, Chung Co," she called. "I'll warn you if it's getting too deep for you." For the first time in her life Hue Hue felt an instinct to protect her brother.

During the next two hours, Hue Hue, up to her neck in water, half wading, half swimming, often wondered whether she would ever reach the white ship. She felt the sea was against her, pushing her small body this way and that. The coral bed hurt her feet, and when the water deepened and she lost her foothold, and her balance too, she reached out vainly for something she might hold onto. She worried about Trung, but consoled herself that as long as her own head remained above water his would be well clear of it. When, long after the men, Hue Hue, Trung, and Binh at last reached the white ship, they were exhausted. Hue Hue was the first to clutch at the end of the rope dangling over the stern; the men aboard began hauling her up. At the top a hand grabbed at hers, but as she held it out, she lost her grip with the other and fell back into the water. At the third attempt, the men managed to haul her aboard. Trung managed more easily. Poor Binh, weak and dispirited, looked as if she would go under, but with Dan's help the rope was fixed under her arms and she was hoisted bodily out of the sea.

While Binh rested, Hue Hue, Trung, Van, and Dan explored the white ship. Long ago it might well have been painted white, but now it was badly eaten by rust and smelled dank with age and corrosion. In the forecastle they found a cabin, triangle shaped, formed by the converging sides of the ship's bow. The door gave aft, straight onto the deck. "Let's make this our home," said Dan. A little farther aft was the hold; of the tarpaulin that had once covered it there remained but a few tattered shreds, leaving the hold gaping open, right down to the bottom of the hull. Farther aft still, the covered wheelhouse sat heavily over the ship's stern. Above it protruded a short mast with a radio antenna stretching from it to a similar mast on the forecastle. Hue Hue, Trung, and the others climbed the narrow companionway that led up to the forecastle. From it they could see the other wreck about two miles away—the black ship, which had been lying there since the year that Trung was born.

That night Hue Hue and the others slept on the iron floor of the triangular cabin. The men had collected shellfish and snails from the reef, and Hue Hue helped Van cook them over a wood fire on the forecastle. With the rice they had brought with them, they ate well. Life did not seem too bad; certainly it was more peaceful aboard the white ship than in the crowded old wooden boat.

During the days that followed, more people kept coming over to the white ship, always at low tide, some men helping the women while others carried the small children on their shoulders. It was a long and dangerous trip across the sharp-edged coral, waist-deep or more in an adverse sea, but every-one managed, and by the end of a week all were safely aboard. Life once more became complicated. The boat people kept to their separate groups—Saigon and Cantho—and within those groups smaller cliques formed. Hue Hue, Trung, Binh, Van, and Dan kept to themselves and watched while the others quarreled over the sharing of food, firewood, the stagnant rainwater lying here and there, the plastic containers with which to catch more—everything necessary to their existence became a cause of dispute.

Little of the rice supply had been salvaged from the boat and the shellfish and snails gathered on the reef provided a meager, unwholesome diet for the fifty half-starved refugees.

A rickety iron ladder ran obliquely halfway down the white ship's starboard side. To its bottom rung the men rigged a rope ladder, made with rope hanging over the stern. This makeshift ladder was now the only way of getting down to the reef and back.

After her crossing from the wooden boat, Hue Hue was in no mind to venture down the ladder. She felt frightened of the sea, as did Trung. Binh had become too weak. Van sometimes went down to the reef, but it was Dan who did most of the foraging for the group, providing them with half a dozen shellfish a day, which had to be dried in the sun after the firewood ran out. With dried shellfish as their only nourishment, the refugees knew that it could not be long before they starved to death. Moreover, their scant, revolting diet was more likely to shorten than prolong their survival, for it created acutely painful gastric disorders. Very soon most of them were suffering from dysentery, which in turn caused dehydration. If only a passing ship would spot them! That was their only chance.

Ladd Reef forms a coral belt enclosing a lagoon whose level rises and falls with the tide breaking across the coral. Beyond the lagoon, on the northwest tip of the reef, lay the wreck of the black ship. Farther still, out to sea, the boat people had seen two or three merchantmen passing. Minh Hung was convinced that the black ship offered the only hope of salvation. From it they would have a better chance of attracting such vessels. He was more right than he knew; the rare ships that did pass that way actually used the black ship as a target to check their radar. Minh Hung and his son-in-law offered to try to cross the lagoon with a small party to investigate the black ship and to base themselves there in the hope of hailing some passing vessel. He called for four unmarried volunteers. Dan was one of them.

The party of six waited until the tide had ebbed and sand

patches were beginning to show in the lagoon; then they climbed down from the white ship onto the coral. The people left aboard watched as they walked toward the lagoon. They saw the men wade into it and, by way of the sand patches, reach the far side. Then the group made toward the black ship, gradually disappearing from view.

Half a week went by; then one afternoon at low tide two figures appeared, wading back across the lagoon. When they came nearer they were recognized as Minh Hung and his son-in-law. Back on board, they told how they had reached the black ship without trouble, except that the lagoon had filled surprisingly fast as soon as the tide turned. After a few days, however, they had begun to worry about their families left behind in the white ship, so they had returned, leaving the four others on board. For the people back in the white ship those four seemed the last hope.

With Dan gone, Hue Hue and her group had lost their provider. Trung, taking his courage in his hands, climbed down the ladder with Van to scour the surrounding coral for shellfish and sea snails. Neither dared go far; the tide was so treacherous. Some days they found none and they and the others had to go hungry. Binh did not seem to mind. She was so weak with hunger and dysentery that she could not face any food at all. Over and over again she would repeat: "Oh, if only I had stayed at home instead of coming here to die. . . ."

Around October 10—Some days after Dan had left them—Hue Hue and Trung were sitting in the shade of the wheelhouse. The heat was intense, but as it began to cool toward the end of the afternoon, the two children got up and strolled forward across the deck. They saw Van hurrying toward them. "Your aunt is very ill," she said and went on to explain that Binh had felt so hot that she wanted to climb down into the sea. "Don't be foolish," Van had told her. "You are sure to drown and no one will try to save you." Binh had lain down again and was now delirious. "Come quickly," Van urged the children. "I am so afraid that Binh is going to die."

Before they reached her the children could hear Binh's cries, wild words that made them stop short, afraid to go to her side. They implored Van to help her; standing a little way off, they watched Van raise Binh's head and put a cup to her lips. But Binh made no attempt to swallow the water, letting it dribble down each side of her mouth.

Two men carried Binh below and for some minutes her delirious ravings echoed from the bottom of the empty hold. Then they faded away and she became silent. Hue Hue, looking down at her, could see that she lay motionless but was still breathing. She knew her aunt needed help but could not summon up enough courage to go to her. Nor could anyone else. If Binh died, she would be the first of them to go; contact with her as she lay in her last agony would bring bad luck. The young woman was left alone. Night fell and no further sound came from her. Hue Hue, believing she was asleep, prayed for her. Early next day she and Trung looked down into the hold. Binh had stopped breathing.

The children were no longer afraid of approaching her. They helped carry her thin, wasted body up on deck and bound it to a plank. Someone took a piece of cloth, wrote on it, and fixed it to Binh's right arm. The message, written in Vietnamese and English, read: "SOS. We are fifty Vietnamese refugees stranded on a reef. SOS." It did not say where the reef was—no one knew—but Buddhists believe that the dead protect the living. Standing beside Binh's corpse, Hue Hue, Trung, and the other mourners prayed that through her influence the message would be answered. Perhaps a passing ship would recover the corpse, perhaps it would float to some inhabited shore.

As the body on its rough bier was lifted and dropped into the sea, Hue Hue covered her face with her hands an turned away. Aunt Binh was so young and had always been good to her. Hue Hue could not bear to watch her body drifting away, alone, on the sea. It was visible for some minutes, and then disappeared forever with its message.

Binh's death and Dan's absence on the black ship brought Trung and Hue Hue even closer. Trung told his sister: "Now you and I are the only ones of the family left aboard. Let's promise always to stick together." "I promise," answered Hue Hue, and Trung said, "I promise too."

10

One evening in mid-October, after curfew had fallen, a smallish white car drew up in front of Tinh's house. Two men got out, one dressed in the light khaki uniform of a police officer with the stripes of chief inspector, the other in plain white shirt and trousers with sandals on his feet. He too was a police officer—of the *mat-vu*, the secret police. Each carried a revolver in a holster attached to his belt.

Tinh had been expecting their visit ever since his elder children's disappearance over a month ago; indeed, he was surprised it had not come sooner. There had been a lot of gossip about them, which must have reached the police through their informers. The school authorities had not contacted Tinh, and he was certain that they had reported Hue Hue and Trung's absence to the police within two or three days.

Tinh appeared quite relaxed as he showed the chief inspector and the plainclothesman into the sitting room. The former began by asking Tinh to show him the householder's register of occupants. Tinh laid it before him; as he examined it, the other man was jotting in a notebook. "And now," asked the inspector, "where are the people corresponding to those on the form?" Le Mai, Quang, and To were presented. "My wife and my two youngest sons," explained Tinh. "And your daughter and elder son?" inquired the inspector. Tinh, ready for that question, replied, "Oh, they left with some friends to go to Saigon." "When did they leave?" "Just under a week ago, at around five in the morning," Tinh replied, knowing well that more than a week's absence had to be reported to the police.

The inspector thought for a moment, then said: "Luong Tinh, I do not believe a word you are saying. You are lying. You know very well that the children escaped more than a month ago. I advise you not to play around with the authorities. If you do, you know what to expect."

Tinh, managing one of his large smiles, apologized. "You know, I have been so worried about them. Yes, I admit I was lying. They left a month ago."

"That's better," said the inspector. "Now sit down and write everything you know in a couple of pages."

Tinh thought hard. He must not make a written confession stating that the children had escaped. To sign anything in the form of a confession was to set a trap for oneself. The authorities had a dossier on Tinh. His confession would be filed and compared in detail with his other papers. The slightest discrepancy, and Tinh would be in for more serious trouble. He was thinking furiously when the inspector interrupted: "If you do not agree to write down all you know, I shall have to take you along with me. Then there will be an official inquiry."

Tinh was cornered. He took a pen and wrote two pages, the gist of his statement being that Hue Hue and Trung had left for Saigon early one morning a month ago with some friends; he had not seen them since. His account bore no resemblance to a confession, nor did Tinh sign it. Handing it to the inspector he asked him: "Will this do?" "Yes, that's okay," replied the police officer.

The plainclothesman now confronted Tinh with a brief, factual statement by the secret police of the children's escape. "Sign it," he ordered, and Tinh refused. "Come on," the man insisted. "And tell us, by the way, how much money did they take with them?"

"Fifty U.S. dollars each," Tinh lied, and the plainclothesman noted that amount on his report.

The inspector spoke: "I advise you to sign the police report, otherwise you will have to come with us." Tinh signed. He would have preferred not to, but at least they were not his own words; it was not a confession on his part. Then the two police officers left.

Tinh knew that from now on, the police would keep a sharper eye than ever on him and his family. Far from deterring him, this made him all the more determined to escape, but after two failures he must make certain of it next time.

Four days after the police visit, an official letter bearing the seal of the War Ministry and addressed to Tran Dieu Trung arrived at Tinh's home. Tinh opened it; inside were his son's call-up papers. He took them immediately to the local recruiting office, where he explained to the *can bo* that his son had escaped and that the police were investigating. The official told him: "All right, forget it; we will keep Tran Dieu Trung's papers on file."

As Tinh and Le Mai had intended, Trung escaped the call-up.

11

Trung at that moment was fighting a battle for survival on Ladd Reef. Death, in the guise of malnutrition and dysentery, had come aboard the white ship to stay. Two days after Binh died, a two-month-old baby succumbed, unable to feed from its mother's breast because there was no milk. The mother died the next day. She and her infant were carried to the ship's side, mourned with a few short prayers, and their bodies cast into the sea.

During those days the tide remained too high for all but the swimmers to search the reef for food. The rope extension of the metal ladder and some of its rungs were below water; it was necessary to swim ashore in a strong swell. Nonswimmers like Trung and weak swimmers like Hue Hue—of which there were many—were confined to the ship. Minh Hung, now that he was no longer on the high seas, had taken over completely from Uncle Ba. He and some of the other veterans encouraged the survivors, especially the youngsters; "Don't sit around doing nothing," they would say. "Keep moving—walk or jog if you can. It is vital if you want to survive."

Minh Hung did not lack courage. Accompanied by his son-in-law and his fourteen-year-old boy, Quan, he swam ashore and foraged far and wide across the coral reef in search of shellfish. When the sea was calm and not too deep, he insisted that his wife and daughter go with him. Minh Hung was the undisputed chief of his clan, to the point of being dictatorial. He was also inclined to be mean. When he and his party returned with their harvest of shellfish, he gave orders that they were to be shared among the family and no one else. His son-in-law, Hue Hue noticed, was quite a different character. The latter befriended her and her brother and obviously wanted to help, despite his father-in-law's orders and the watchful eye of his own wife. With the help of his two sisters, nonswimmers like Trung and Hue Hue, he circumvented Minh Hung's orders. As soon as the foraging party was out of sight, the two kind sisters supplied the children from the family store—until, after some days, they had no more to give.

This latter moment coincided, luckily, with a period of low tide. Trung and Hue Hue plucked up their courage, and they and Van climbed down the ladder on to the coral to hunt for shellfish. Because they dreaded being cut off by the tide that came sweeping in over the coral at a frightening speed, they dared not wander far from the ship. The area had been well scoured in recent days; few shellfish remained, and the hunters often went hungry.

No one had forgotten the four men, Dan among them, on board the black ship stranded at the northwest tip of the reef. Some of the hardier young men made several attempts to reach it, but the lagoon that lay between it and the white ship at the southern end of the reef proved a most treacherous obstacle. Those left behind on the white ship watched the men as they waded some way into the lagoon, took fright, and, half-wading, half-swimming, regained the near shore. Finally, five men succeeded in crossing to the other side of the lagoon. They forged their way on toward the black ship, all the time glancing back at the incoming tide, until they stopped some way short of the wreck, waving and shouting. No answer came from the black ship—save one that they well understood. A flock of seagulls rose, wheeled, and settled again. That, they believed, could mean only one thing: there was not a living person aboard.

They turned immediately and hurried back. The tide was already sweeping across the coral into the lagoon. The five men plunged into the water and swam. Vainly they searched for the sand patches that had been there an hour before. They struggled on against the swirling tide, toward the other side. Only three of them reached it and, farther on, the white ship.

With a prayer for his soul, Trung and Hue Hue mourned the death of their cousin Dan. Thereafter the children never left one another's side; they strolled on deck, avoiding the hold where Binh had died, and stared over the side, watching the sea roll toward the ship, beat against it, and retreat. They gazed toward the horizon and their thoughts journeyed on to Vietnam, to Cantho, their house, their parents and young brothers. At night Hue Hue and Trung, lying beside one another on the cabin floor, their stomachs aching with emptiness, would talk of their favorite dishes: *banh zeo* and *banh khot, cha gia, chao gao,* and *nem nuong.* The taste of them came back, and in the dark they would smile and feel almost satisfied. With such pleasant thoughts in mind, they would fall asleep. But never for long. In the darkness, night after night, they awakened to the sound of delirious cries, heard hoarsely whispered, fervent prayers, a final, halting breath. Then there would be silence. Next morning the body, sometimes two or three, would be dragged across the deck and heaved overboard without ceremony into the sea.

Dysentery was ravaging the company aboard the white ship. No one could tell who was going to die next, nor even be sure who it was who had last died. Uncle Ba just disappeared—neither Trung nor Hue Hue saw him go. Minh Hung was found one morning by his son, Quan, at the bottom of the hold. Dysentery and exhaustion made short shrift of all the rest of his family except Quan. Hue Hue and Trung felt a vague gratitude and regret for Minh Hung's son-in-law and the sisters who had been so kind to them. But they lacked the strength to grieve more.

The people aboard the white ship were caught up in a macabre process in which the ladder down the ship's side played a vital part. It led down to blue-green sea breaking white on a pink coral strand—the very image of a desert island paradise; it led up to a hell of dysentery, detritus, and stinking death. The ladder provided the only access to the meager food supply, but as the people aboard weakened, they found it more and more difficult to climb down. Finally it became impossible for most of them. Thereafter they became prisoners on the white ship, condemned to death. There was another ironic aspect to the ladder. Those who managed to negotiate it returned with food, it was true, but it was food that brought a little life to some and death to others. Not all could stomach those foul sea snails and shellfish, which poisoned them, caused dysentery, and hastened them to an agonizing death. Some who managed to get down the ladder, gather their shellfish, and return to the double rope and crosspieces dangling before them found that they lacked the strength to climb up again. They collapsed on the coral reef, and their wasted, feeble bodies were swept away on the next tide.

Aboard the ship itself, the dying had to bury their dead in the sea, dragging them to the ship's side with what strength remained to them.

Some chose to end their lives by throwing themselves down to the bottom of the hold, some thirty feet below. The rectangular hole was surrounded by a protective railing. Those who were too weak to climb it collapsed across it, head downward, and died there. Others, bent on throwing themselves overboard, were too feeble to reach the ship's side. They collapsed on deck and died where they lay.

The youngest of the boat people still surviving was thirteen-year-old Hue Hue. Death no longer frightened her, but she was determined, almost aggressively, not to let it beat her. She often had to help with the dismal chore of dragging bodies to burial in the sea. Never, she said to herself, was anyone going to drag *her* dead body across the deck and drop it overboard. Her mind, the whole of her small being, was concentrated on survival. Unlike her, Trung became resigned. "We all have to die one day," he said to Hue Hue.

After Binh's death, Hue Hue had quickly accepted the situation and had accustomed herself to live with death, until the sight and smell of it no longer registered on her mind. Others might take things differently; that was their problem. She would help them if they needed her, but she could not change them. Since she had been aboard the white ship, Hue Hue had never failed, night after night, to go up on the forecastle after sunset and pray: for her family, for her brother Trung and herself; again and again, "Oh, God, oh, Buddha, please send us help, a ship to save us."

Hue Hue could never forget how every evening at home she had gone around the household shrines, lighting joss sticks and praying. To her prayer was a habit, and she believed in its power. She had often been aware that her prayers, childlike as they were, had been answered. The answer was not always what she expected, it was true, but she had at least gotten the feeling that she had been heard. She believed she always would be.

At the beginning many others prayed with her on the

forecastle. Death thinned their numbers to a dozen, to half a dozen, to two or three, until through sickness or loss of faith, no one else came. Trung was no longer there but not because he had lost faith; he was just too weak to move. "Let me lie here and pray," he said one evening to Hue Hue. "Let me rest, and when I am stronger I will go again with you." Hue Hue took his hand and held it for an instant; then she climbed up the companionway to the forecastle.

The sun had set some time ago, the sky was full of color and glory, and stars were coming out. Hue Hue felt close to eternity and, in her terrible distress, close to God. She knelt on the iron deck, still warm from the departed sun, looked up at the heavens, and prayed. When she had finished, bowing until her forehead touched the deck, she sat up, arranged herself cross-legged, and closed her eyes. For some minutes she remained thus, in contemplation. Then she rose and walked slowly back down the companionway to her cabin.

Ever since Trung had remarked, "We all have to die one day," he had been a source of anxiety to his young sister. She suspected that his gentle assurances were mainly intended to encourage her and feared that he had neither the physical strength nor the will to survive. His slight frame was ravaged with sickness; dysentery and the gnawing pangs of hunger left him in ceaseless, acute pain. Hue Hue encouraged him: "Come on, Chung Co, try to get up and walk a little." Trung always answered, "I'm all right lying down. I'm waiting to get stronger, then I'll walk." Patiently, day after day, Hue Hue kept trying to coax her brother, until at last he made the effort. Helped by her, he rose and, steadying himself against her, tried to walk. Hue Hue led him very slowly outside on the deck where she sat him down. For the first time in days he breathed fresh air and seemed to be the better for it. But Hue

Hue could no longer deceive herself. The thought that he would probably die made her very afraid.

During the next few days Trung lay in the cabin, unwilling to move. More than once Hue Hue heard him say that he wanted to throw himself down into the hold. "There are so many people dying," he went on, murmuring to himself, "and I'm surely going to be one of them." Then to Hue Hue he said: "I don't want to die the same way as Aunt Binh; I don't want to make trouble for the others. I can't bear the thought of you, little Hue Hue, having to drag my dead body to the side and throw me into the sea."

Their friend Van was listening. She took Hue Hue aside and said: "Your brother is suffering terribly—in his mind and in his body. Everything he says makes me sure that he will try to end his life. He thinks that if he does this he will be sparing you further pain. You must stay with him all the time; never take your eyes off him."

It was mid-November, and there were now fewer than a score of people alive. Hue Hue never left her brother's side. She nursed him with all the care and tenderness she could muster in hellish conditions; talked to him about the family and home and food, of the fun they had had on the Honda, of the movies they had seen together, of dancing and table tennis and weekends at Vung Tau—anything to distract him. She spoke to him too, seriously, about his talk of jumping into the hold. "That is an idea you must put clean out of your head," Hue Hue told her brother firmly. Desperately ill as he was, Trung never ceased to cherish his sister; he murmured back: "Don't worry, little Hue Hue, I have no intention of doing any such thing."

Trung lingered on in his sister's care for another week. Then one morning Hue Hue woke up suddenly. Trung was just outside the cabin, half-crawling, half-dragging himself across the deck. "Chung Co, where are you going?" Hue Hue called after him, and Trung replied, "To the toilet." "All right, Chung Co, wait; I'm coming to help you." When Hue Hue reached her brother, he had already crossed the deck and was near the place in the stern where they first climbed aboard two months ago. Hue Hue knew well her brother's logical mind. She placed herself between him and the side of the ship and asked reproachfully: "Chung Co, what are you trying to do? Were you going to throw yourself over? Tell me," she repeated, "were you going to throw yourself over?" Exhausted by his effort, Trung answered, "No, Hue Hue, no. I won't do that."

A sudden thought came to Hue Hue. Looking into the tired, inflamed eyes of her brother she said slowly: "Listen, Chung Co. When Aunt Binh died we promised each other that we would always stick together. Promise me that again!" Trung did not reply. After a moment he said, "I'm hungry, Hue Hue. Please try and find me a little food." Was this, she wondered, an attempt to distract her attention? "You really want me to?" she asked, a trace of doubt in her voice. "Yes, Hue Hue, really."

Hue Hue looked around. At the other end of the ship, on the forecastle, two people were laying out their shellfish to dry. "All right," she said. "Stay there and don't move. I'll be right back." She ran toward the forecastle, unsteadily climbed the companionway. The two people looked up. "Please," she asked them, "may I have something for my brother—he's very hungry." One of them answered peevishly, "Why do you keep bothering us? You were here only yesterday and back you come again today." "But my brother . . ." Hue Hue pleaded with them, and they gave her a single, half-dried shellfish.

She thanked them and turned to rejoin Trung, whom she had left sitting on deck near the stern. As she came to the top of the companionway, Hue Hue saw with horror that he was now on his feet, leaning over the ship's side. She half-climbed, half-fell down the narrow iron ladder. Then she began to run, calling him by name: "Chung Co, Chung Co, don't! Don't do it!" Trung ignored her. He continued to work the upper part of his body over the side until he overbalanced and fell toward the sea.

Hue Hue screamed for help. Reaching the stern she looked over and saw Trung struggling feebly in the water. A minute later he disappeared. Hue Hue turned away, sat down on the deck and, her head buried in her folded arms, sobbed, feeling she could never stop. People came to her as fast as their feeble legs would carry them. They spoke comfortingly to her. "This was his wish," they said. "He has gone to heaven more quickly. He wanted to do it," they kept saying. "It was his wish."

But it was not hers. Cut off as she was from the rest of her family, she had needed Trung to fill all their places. He had become everything to her. Now that she had lost him, she had lost her entire family. She was left utterly, desolately alone.

For days, her loneliness was the only thought that occupied Hue Hue's mind. It preyed on her and, unable to rid herself of it, she cried continuously. Through crying, she became weaker than ever; but that, she reflected, was at least an advantage for the others, because she made less noise.

Then gradually, as she thought more about it, Hue Hue began to see Trung's death as a challenge to her. She recalled that Trung, knowing he was dying, had asked her always to remember the anniversary of his death—about the twenty-second day of November, 1978—and to pray for him at the temple and make an offering. If she were to die too, how could she keep her promise? Who would be left to pray for her beloved brother?

12

The inquiries that Tinh had addressed to his friends in Manila, Sydney, and Malaysia about his missing children had so far produced no response. Over two months had passed since Trung and Hue Hue had disappeared, and, though Tinh never abandoned hope, he had to be honest with himself and admit that little chance remained of ever hearing of them again.

It was an ironic coincidence that within a day or two of his eldest son's death, Tinh made the move that would eventually provide him with news of Trung and Hue Hue. On November 23 he, Le Mai, and their two boys, and another fifteen families—some fifty people in all—piled into a private coach Tinh had chartered and discreetly parked near the market-place. Their destination was Ca Mau, a port at the extreme southwestern tip of Vietnam, about a hundred miles away, or, allowing for police checks, about three and a half hours' drive.

Tinh had begun preparing for his third escape attempt immediately after the police investigation into the disappearance of his two elder children. He decided this time to do everything possible to reduce the chance of another failure to a minimum. The government had recently begun to consent to "assisted" escapes—an operation reserved exclusively for ethnic Chinese. For the government it was an excellent deal; it provided a convenient way of getting rid of the Chinese and at the same time ensured that the refugees, instead of smuggling out their money in the form of gold bars, jewelry, and dollar bills, were stripped of the lot at the final police checkpoint.

The Vietnamese government in fact was now engaged in a scandalous trade, in which the merchandise consisted of persecuted human beings. The Chinese were being exported to unspecified destinations in neighboring Asian countries. For the government, or more exactly its local representatives, the trade was proving highly lucrative, the price exacted greatly exceeding the cost of a clandestine escape. Tinh himself had to put down more than thirty ounces troy of gold for the three "units" in his family—himself, his wife, and the two little boys, who counted as half a unit each. A typical boatload of four hundred refugees, comprising around three hundred units, brought in a hundred kilos (250 pounds troy) of gold.

The "assisted" escape operation was unofficial yet approved by the national authorities. Its execution was left to the government agencies in each of six provincial capitals: Cantho, Ca Mau, Pac Nieu, Rach Gia, Ben Tre, and My Tho. Though the phrase "assisted" meant tacitly approved by the provincial government concerned, it did not provide an absolute guarantee of security. If en route to the port of departure the refugee had to pass through another province and was apprehended by their police, or if on the high seas he was intercepted by a naval patrol—that was his bad luck. The penalty was then the same as if he had been making a clandestine escape, though a hefty bribe could often settle matters.

Considering his record with the Cantho province police, Tinh decided on Ca Mau as the point of departure. It was the nearest port to the Malaysian coast, some three hundred miles to the southwest. Tinh had a good friend living in Ca Mau, a

Chinese named Ban who was on excellent terms with the local police. Another convenient feature about the town was that it was in a region famous for its rice. This provided a plausible cover story. While organizing the escape, Tinh had to make many trips from Cantho to Ca Mau; if questioned at any one of the four police checkpoints en route, he could plead that he was traveling for the same reason as most people who went to Ca Mau—to buy rice.

Between mid-October and mid-November Tinh made eight trips by country bus to Ca Mau. He would leave on the first bus and try to return to Cantho the same evening. Only rarely did he stay overnight, for he dared not risk the police noticing a longer absence from his workshop. To Le Mai and the children he never mentioned Ca Mau. The rice he managed to explain away, or sometimes he gave it to someone else before reaching home. Le Mai and the children were instructed to reply, if questioned, "He's gone to Saigon on business." And Tinh, while not journeying to and fro, was indeed very busy, for he needed more money to pay for the escape.

On his first visit to Ca Mau, Tinh spent the day with his friend Ban, discussing the broad outline of the operation and Tinh's particular responsibility, which was to make contact with fifteen families in Cantho and arrange for them to be brought to Ca Mau on the required date. Tinh was also to obtain and store in the boat enough food and medicines for the fifty-odd people of his group. Another vital job he undertook was to ensure that sufficient diesel fuel was stowed aboard. Here he would have to work closely with the police. The next visit would have to be devoted to them. Meanwhile Tinh, with his bag of rice, hurried back to Cantho and got on with his watch repairing.

Some days later he again took the early morning bus to Ca Mau. As his friend Ban took him along to police headquarters, Tinh felt nervous. Ban reassured him: "Don't worry, these men are good types. They're mostly Vietnamese, but there are a few Chinese. They're only interested in the cut they're going to get. You'll see, Tinh, you'll soon find them the best of friends." And so they proved to be, these officers of the law, who were bending it as far as they could so as to ensure a good deal for the boat people and a far better one for the state. Tinh was the first to admit that it was a dirty business; but it was the safest way of getting out.

Tinh's first interview with the police went smoothly. With his friend Ban proposing himself as guarantor, Tinh undertook to pay, as soon as he had collected it, the "fare" of his group—some forty pounds troy of solid gold. The discussion continued pleasantly, and when every detail had been settled, the police chief said, "Two of my men will accompany you to inspect the boat." He made it sound as if the boat belonged to him, which, in a way, it did. The original owner had been black-mailed into selling his boat to the provincial government; the price offered was well below its value, but when he remonstrated he was told by the *can bo*: "That is the government's price. Accept it or we confiscate your boat." The assisted-escape program had to show a profit for the government.

The boat, which bore the register number MH0126, was moored to a jetty in the nearby river, the Song Doc, which led into the estuary. From there it was a half mile to the sea. The boat was seventy-five feet long and twenty-one feet across the beam. Solidly built, it was powered by two six-cylinder diesel engines of American manufacture as well as an auxiliary motor. Tinh was impressed, but at the same time he remembered how Le Mai had reproached him for allowing his elder children to risk their lives in that other broken-down old tub. He felt bitterly remorseful. Tinh tried not to think of what had become of Trung and Hue Hue.

Tinh made another half-dozen visits to Ca Mau without incident, purchasing on-the-spot stores, medicines, and fuel and arranging for them to be stowed aboard. The police were always helpful, amiable even, and Tinh in return would buy them beer or invite them to eat with him, half a dozen or a dozen at a time. They were delighted to be regaled so generously with food, drink, and cigarettes.

By mid-November everything was ready, and the departure date from Cantho was fixed for November 23. At a little after eleven that morning, the family, those departing and those remaining, met for the last time near Tinh's house. If the farewell was not quite so painful this time—the abortive effort of two months ago had helped to accustom them to the idea— the two grandmothers were once more in tears. The very fact that this escape looked so sure of success made it as good as certain that they would never again see their children and grandchildren.

In the discreet way of the Vietnamese, the two grandmothers in turn clasped the hands of Le Mai and Tinh, of Quang and To. Phuong, Le Mai's sister, and Ngan, Tinh's sister, did the same. Then the four women walked dejectedly back to their homes, while Tinh and his family made ready to leave. They bade good-bye to the housekeeper with the same instruction as before: "Help yourself to anything you want." Then they closed the front door behind them. Phuong's husband, Hinh, and Hien, the husband of Ngan, were waiting on their Hondas. The two boys jumped up behind Hinh, and the motorscooter buzzed away toward the waiting coach. With them went their mother, on the back of Hien's Honda. Hien was soon back to fetch Tinh.

In the side street where the coach was parked, other families were arriving. An hour later, at one o'clock, it left, driven by a trusted friend of Tinh's. No one carried any luggage save a small plastic bag containing the bare necessities for a one-night stay at Ca Mau that would not make the police along the route suspicious. But all of them, old and young, had hidden about them a supply of money in some form or another. Tinh himself carried ten ounces troy of gold leaf; Le Mai wore a gold necklace, the two little boys each a gold ring. At the approach to the four police checkpoints everyone's heart beat hard enough almost to rock the bus, but they got by each time without incident. Fortunately there was a lot of traffic. The policeman simply asked the driver, "Where are you going with that lot?" "They're all going on a family outing to Ca Mau, to buy rice," the driver replied, and the policeman waved them on.

Before the driver left on the return trip to Cantho, Tinh asked him to call on the two grandmothers and tell them that the family had arrived safely. It was many days before the message was delivered. At the first police checkpoint Tinh's friend was asked to explain how he came to be driving an empty coach back to Cantho. He was detained some days while an investigation was made, though finally he got off with a fine of seventy *dong*—about $35.

Tihh himself could thank God that he and his family were, for the time being, safe. He had previously arranged lodgings at Ca Mau for them and for the other families of the group. He felt satisfied. The first lap of the journey to freedom was over and all had gone well. He and the others were now under the benevolent care of the Ca Mau police. Tinh could relax as he waited for the boat's departure to Malaysia, due in a couple of weeks when police formalities would be completed.

13

On Ladd Reef, six hundred miles away in the opposite direction, Tinh's daughter Hue Hue sat crying on the floor of her cabin. For days now, since Trung's death, she had cried every morning when she woke up and found he was not there and in the evening as she went to sleep. Repelled by the changeless, unappetizing diet of dried shellfish, she grew thinner than ever, and weaker too.

At the death of Trung, fifteen of the original fifty boat people remained alive. In Hue Hue's cabin there were four: an old lady, Hue Hue's friend, Van, and Hue Hue. At night Hue Hue's sobbing was heard less and less, the delirious cries of the sick more and more. The cries did not disturb her; she had become used to these lugubrious sounds at night. During the three weeks that followed Trung's death, eight more of the fifteen survivors died. Van was the eighth. Lying next to Hue Hue, she had begun to cry out wildly. Her delirium lasted nearly a week; then one morning Hue Hue found her dead. After all Van's kindness to her and the affection she felt for her friend, it hurt Hue Hue to help in the rude, impious burial, but it had to be done. Holding the end of one of Van's arms, she and three others dragged the cold body across the deck and dropped it into the sea.

110

Each one of the survivors counted the days as they passed. If one forgot or mistook the date, someone else would remind him of it. All the same, as the survivors became fewer and weaker, time meant less and less to them.

Van's death, about mid-December, reduced the number of survivors to seven. There was Huong, a woman of thirty; and another, Lan, aged twenty; and Cuong, a youth of nineteen— all belonging to the Saigon group and sharing a separate cabin. In the Cantho group, who bedded down in Hue Hue's triangular cabin in the bow, there was Quan, Minh Hung's fourteen-year-old son, and his nineteen-year-old sister-in-law, Mai, with whom Hue Hue had been friendly ever since she had secretly given Hue Hue and Trung shellfish caught by the Minh Hung family.

The fourth member of the Cantho group sharing Hue Hue's cabin was Tai, a youth of eighteen. These four teenagers had become close friends who felt more like brothers and sisters. They talked among themselves about anything and everything—except death. Close as it was to them all, death was never mentioned. Hue Hue prayed every day—she was the only one to do so—but she was too weak now to go up onto the forecastle. She prayed where she sat, leaning against the cabin wall.

The members of the Saigon group were, on the whole, older. The two groups had never gotten on well, despite their common plight, but now with death so close they agreed that it was worth one more attempt to reach the black ship and attract the attention of a passing merchantman. So hopeful were they that they burdened themselves with an odd assortment of baggage—bundles of clothes and sandals, most of them belonging to the dead. Hue Hue had already lost her own sandals with their hidden five *la* of gold leaf, but she did not care; gold was no good to anyone on Ladd Reef. She now wore sandals whose owner had no further use for them.

The party waited for low tide, then one by one the seven of them summoned the strength to climb carefully down the rickety metal ladder, onto the rope extension. Some minutes later they all stood on the dry coral. Led by fourteen-year-old Quan, who had often ventured far afield looking for shellfish, they set off toward the lagoon and the black ship beyond. Before they had gone far, they found that the baggage was slowing them up, especially Hue Hue, who was carrying some of Mai's as well as her own. Anxious to press on, they threw most of it away.

When they waded into the lagoon they realized immediately that not only had their progress been too slow, but they had waited too long before starting. The tide had already turned and, helped by a fresh breeze, was rising fast and filling the lagoon. They struggled, nearly waist deep, to the first sand patch, but there Quan gave up. "I'm not going on," he told the others. "I'd rather die here or in the white ship than try to go farther." Mai and Tai felt the same; the Cantho group were all turning back, except for Hue Hue, who agreed with the Saigon people that they should push on. They stood and argued as the sea rose and broke around them, until at last all agreed to turn back.

Hue Hue was up to her waist in the rough, choppy sea; but it was the sharp, uneven coral bed that most impeded her. She fell several times, cutting her knee and both legs. The others, though taller than she, were struggling as hard. Somehow Hue Hue reached the white ship. She was the first to grab the rope ladder, the end of which was being dragged here and there by the waves breaking against the ship. To be in front of someone at the ladder was a considerable help, for the next person held it steady. It was the last one to climb the ladder who had the most difficulty. Hue Hue hauled herself up, followed by the others. Last came Mai and Tai, both exhausted. They grabbed at the ladder, but it drifted past them. Again they grabbed and again, but each time it evaded them. Then a big wave broke over them and carried them farther out. Weakened beyond further resistance, Mai and Tai disappeared without struggle.

There now remained five survivors. In the Cantho group there was Hue Hue and Quan. Huong, Lan, and young Cuong of the Saigon group suggested the two parties should join up, and they came into the triangular cabin. Immediately Huong and Lan began to boss the others around. They were aggressive and greedy (insofar as there was anything to be greedy about), and ceaselessly made trouble with the young ones, who, after two days, told them firmly to return to their own cabin. Hue Hue and Quan were glad to see the last of the two women. Young Cuong, however, asked to stay with the Cantho children, and they happily agreed. He got on well with them now that the two women had left. The two boys slept on one side of the cabin, Hue Hue on the other. Quan sometimes talked sadly of his dead parents. One day he climbed down into the hold and returned with a plastic bag full of bones. He had taken them from the feet of his father's body, now dried out to a skeleton. Reverently Quan stacked his father's bones in a neat little heap by the side of his sleeping mat. After that he was no longer as sad.

After their ill-fated attempt to reach the black ship, the five survivors dared not again descend the ladder to search for food. They did not have the strength—still less to climb up again onto the deck of the white ship. They were too weak even to move more than a few yards. Quan could no longer get to his feet and had to crawl; the others, supporting themselves against the cabin wall or some other prop, moved only if they had to and then slowly and unsteadily. Most of the day they sat silent and motionless, waiting for the end. Hue Hue was still the only one who prayed. Propped against the cabin wall, she begged: "Send a ship, or let us die quickly."

Some fifteen miles away to the east of Ladd Reef lies Spratly Island. It is surrounded by white sand and broken coral and dotted with a few palm trees. As Captain Spratly had reported over a century earlier, the island was "inhabited by thousands of the feathered tribe." It still is. Its only other occupants are the three-hundred-odd soldiers of the Republic of Vietnam's garrison. Members of the Vietnamese garrison on another island, Pugad, earned for themselves the name "the Brutes of Pugad." They lined up on the beach and massacred in cold blood over one hundred boat people who had the misfortune to run aground there. Mercifully, military garrisons are not in the habit of wandering far from their base; otherwise the Spratly garrison might have discovered the boat people on nearby Ladd Reef and, like the Brutes of Pugad, murdered them all.

Seabirds, however, do move around in search of better feeding grounds and shelter, and this fact led to a small miracle occurring before the eyes of the five survivors as they awaited death. No doubt lured by the apparent lack of life aboard the wreck, first one seagull, then another, then crowds more, came planing down one evening to roost. They perched on the roof of the wheelhouse, the deck of the poop, the forecastle, the side of the ship—anywhere flat. Finally, one by one, each twisted its neck around and dug its beak under one wing. A few remained to watch. They were a potential source of food to replace the shellfish out of reach on the coral reef.

When Hue Hue was very little, she had often watched the

seagulls wheeling above the riverside near her home at Cantho. Now, because her survival depended on the gulls, she watched them far more closely as they made their home on the white ship. She sat at the entrance to her cabin, back against the outer wall, facing the stern. There she stayed, from half an hour before sunset until dark, observing the seagulls as they came flying in. She watched them with admiration, because they looked so beautiful; but her aim was that of a hunter. She noticed that when the birds flew across the ship they never landed; it was when they overflew the ship lengthwise that they glided down. Some landed on the forecastle behind her, where she could not see them, others on the poop in front of her, where she was able to observe and count them. With time she was to discover a lot more about seagull hunting, but her first attempt was amateurish. If the boys had had their way there would not even have been such an attempt. When Hue Hue said she was ready to help, Cuong and Quan laughed at her.

"You're a girl! You'll never catch a seagull; it takes a man to do a job like that." They went out on deck to take up their positions. Hue Hue waited in the cabin until the boys came back, each with a seagull. "Congratulate us, Hue Hue," Cuong said. "Tomorrow morning, as soon as it's light, it'll be your turn to work—to pluck and clean them and lay them out to dry." Until then they would all have to go hungry.

Cuong and Quan lay down, lulling themselves to sleep with talk of their prowess as seagull hunters, while Hue Hue listened. When they fell silent, she slipped out of the cabin and across the deck toward the stern, where she had marked her seagulls. Very slowly, she crept on all fours toward the nearest one. Measuring her distance, an arm's length, she pounced and grabbed it by a wing, while the other birds flew off screaming into the dark. Hue Hue managed to hold both flapping wings of her bird as it jabbed at her arms with its beak, drawing blood. Clumsily she crossed the bird's wings and held them by their roots, while with her other hand she held the gull's head to prevent it from lacerating her arms. Then, with her squawking, terrified prey, she made her way carefully back to the cabin. The boys, startled, woke up to hear Hue Hue asking: "Who said I couldn't catch a seagull?" Quan lay back and closed his eyes again. "No, Hue Hue," she heard him murmur. "No, I don't believe it." She fastened her bird with string by one leg, like the others. None had the strength to wring its neck.

In the daylight next morning the two boys had to accept the proof of Hue Hue's skill. All three now took part in the hunt, stationing themselves well before sunset in positions where they could cover most of the deck. The quarter of an hour before sunset was the critical time, when the seagulls overflew the white ship, reconnoitering their perch for the night. From then until dark the three hunters remained motionless, marking their birds. After dark they met once more in the cabin to get some sleep, while the seagulls, outside, did the same.

The constant sound of the sea, whether the crash of breaking waves or the murmur as it rippled over the coral, kept the youngsters on the *qui vive*. They were hunters, waiting for the moment to strike at their prey, to kill for food. All three slept lightly and there was always one of them, usually Hue Hue, who woke up and roused the others some hours after darkness. Then they would wrap themselves against the cold in such scanty clothing as they possessed and go out into the dark to take up their stations. Their tactics, at first far from perfectly synchronized, improved steadily; soon it was rare for one of them to return empty-handed—unless that night, for some reason, there were no seagulls to catch. Then they went hungry and drank rainwater instead. On a normal night, with two well-spaced sorties, they would each bring in two birds, screaming, pecking, clawing, unable to break free from the hand gripping the roots of their wings. Back in the cabin the wings were bound fast while a string was attached to the bird's leg. By morning the bird was usually dead—if not, its head was knocked against the cabin wall. It was a cruel and undeserved fate for a graceful white seagull; but for those aboard the white ship, fate was still more cruel.

14

It was the turn of the year. Hue Hue's birthday had just passed, almost without her noticing it. When, on the evening of December 28, it struck her that she was fourteen that day, she thought momentarily of the party she would have been having at home. Immediately she shut her mind to the idea. At present, catching seagulls was more important.

Early in the morning a couple of days later, Lan, the younger of the Saigon women, came to Hue Hue's cabin in great distress. Her companion, Huong, had died during the night. Huong was thirty. She and Lan—the last of the Saigon group—had been holding out alone in their cabin on part of the proceeds of the Cantho group's seagull-hunting. In return they had undertaken to pluck, clean, and dry the birds. But the meager, unbalanced diet of dried seagull meat proved insufficient to sustain the five survivors indefinitely. However strong the will to hold on, it gradually lost its power in a body that, through malnutrition, was ceasing to function. Huong's body had not resisted. She was the first on the seagull diet to succumb. Lan, despite her grief, helped the others to drag Huong's body across the deck to its final resting place in the sea below.

Another week passed while Lan, who had now joined the other three in their cabin, cried most days and only picked disgustedly at the dried seagull meat. Then one morning she announced, "I cannot stay here any longer. I'm going over to the black ship. Please, please come with me," she implored the other three. Hue Hue could only reply truthfully: "It's too far, and I'm too frightened of the sea. I'm staying here. Stay with us, Lan. We can help each other." Lan knew her entreaties were useless; Cuong and Quan could hardly walk across the deck to the ladder, let alone tackle the dangerous journey across the lagoon.

Alone, she began to descend the ladder, barely keeping her balance. She reached the coral and began walking. Watching her, Hue Hue could see that Lan held out no more hope for life; her head bent low, often losing her foothold, she was walking voluntarily to her death. Hue Hue followed the receding figure until Lan reached the lagoon and waded straight in. She faded into a distant speck and then vanished beneath the water.

It was one afternoon in early January 1979 that Lan disappeared. Weak as they were, Cuong, Quan and Hue Hue were hardly moved. Emotions like grief and anger no longer troubled them. They felt no pain, either, the worst pangs of hunger being assuaged by the seagull meat. The mind of each was centered on one thing—food. They felt close to one another, those three teenagers who such a short while before had been thinking only of their studies, of music and fun, but to whom now only one thing mattered. As they lay waiting for sleep, they always talked, usually of food, sometimes of home. In her prayers, which she said aloud, and in her conversation, Hue Hue made no secret to the boys that she would never cease to believe that a boat would one day come to save them. She said two prayers. The first went, "Please God, send a boat

119

to save us"; the second, "If you aren't going to send a boat, then please don't keep us suffering like this for too long. Please let us die, soon." She was not losing hope, but felt that it was only rational to admit the possibility that relief might never come. The boys listened, but they could not share her confidence that a boat would appear. "Hue Hue, we admire your faith, but it's no use," said Cuong. "We're finished . . . but we're not at all scared." Quan agreed.

As she slept, Hue Hue often dreamed. Night after night she dreamed of home, of her father and mother and her two grandmothers, or her brothers Quang and To and Trung. Trung was always there with the family. She dreamed of Co Ut cooking a wonderful meal; Hue Hue could smell it, taste it. Everyone was laughing and eating, and she heard her father say: "Hue Hue, eat up; you must eat well because we're going to the boat." Hue Hue would see herself walking down to the boat. Her sandals seemed heavy and kept slipping off. Then the dream would end and Hue Hue would wake up in the dark. The truth would hit her with a thud; she was lying on the hard floor of the cabin in the white ship; her family was nowhere near; and she was starving to death.

Both the boys were now very weak and the exertion of catching seagulls was beyond them. Every night Hue Hue did the hunting while the boys, propped against the cabin wall, plucked the seagulls and cleaned them. Hue Hue would then spread the birds to dry on deck—the process needed half a day or so. When there were no birds to eat, water was the only substitute. It helped a little to quell the pangs of hunger.

Hue Hue's cunning grew. Since her first clumsy efforts she had learned many things. Seagulls, she realized, could see only sideways. The easiest way of catching one was to creep up on it from behind; the next best approach was from dead ahead. A lone bird with its one pair of eyes was an easier target than one of a group with their several pairs. She discovered that birds, like soldiers camping for the night, had sentinels posted at several points; she had to be wary of these or they would scream an alarm and the rest would flap off into the dark. Moonless nights favored the little hunter. Despite the dark, Hue Hue could see the white silhouette of her prey while she, in her ragged black trousers and checked jacket, remained invisible. The brighter the moon, the more difficult was stalking. She would then take care to pick a bird perched above her so that, as she crept in for the kill, flattened against the deck, dragging herself on her elbows, inching toward it, she would avoid being silhouetted against the moonlit sky.

Hue Hue no longer pounced on her prey. She moved stealthily, imperceptibly, until within an arm's length of it. Only then, as a water snake grabs a basking frog, did Hue Hue make the lightning stroke, grasping the head and beak if she could to neutralize the bird's defense, and with her other hand ·seizing the thrashing wings. She dreaded the beak, those powerful yellow pincers that stabbed at her bone-thin arm and sometimes closed on the whole of it, slashing a bleeding wound halfway around it. But as Hue Hue's skill increased, she usually managed to avoid getting hurt—except when she tried to bag two birds at once. The night's bag never exceeded two birds, for at each attack all the others flew off screaming to the safety of the coral. It was a long wait before they returned to the ship. Hue Hue would return to the cabin and there tie up her bird, its wings trussed and a string fixed to its leg.

Seagulls were not the only birds that came to roost on the white ship. Others, smaller, plumper, and colored a reddish brown, arrived in large droves. What were they? Pigeons of a kind, sand plovers, puffins, petrels? Hue Hue had no idea; to her they looked like pigeons. Before the boys became too weak, they and Hue Hue caught these birds not singly but by armfuls, as many as twelve in a night. Though smaller, these birds were more meaty and tasty than the seagulls, which, once stripped of their immaculate white plumage, were but a handful of skin and bones.

The boys' strength was ebbing so that they could no longer manage even the effort of plucking and cleaning the birds. They would start the job propped up against the cabin wall, then give up and slide down into a lying position. Hue Hue now had to do everything to keep them fed—catching the birds, plucking, cleaning, and drying them; then brushing the cabin floor and the surrounding deck clean of feathers and entrails, and finally feeding the sun-dried flesh to her companions. She still managed to walk slowly, placing one foot deliberately before the other, occasionally leaning on some convenient prop.

She often glanced at the elder boy, Cuong. Though slightly more active than Quan, he looked hideously thin, his eyes sunk into his head, the skin of his face drawn tightly across his cheekbones leaving his teeth partially bared. One night Cuong died, silently; and in the morning Hue Hue and Quan—the boy was so weak that his help was negligible—each holding the end of one arm, somehow managed to get Cuong's body to the side and over it into the sea.

Hue Hue helped Quan back to the cabin, where they both lay down exhausted, Hue Hue in her usual place, Quan in his, next to the stack of his father's bones. For some time they did not speak. Then Quan said slowly: "You know, Hue Hue, I'm not frightened during the day. What really scares me are the nights. I'm afraid of ghosts and evil spirits." Hue Hue remembered the time when she, too, had been tormented by such visions. "I used to be frightened, too, when I was little," she answered, "but my father said there was nothing to be afraid of. Now I know he was right." Quan said nothing, and a moment later Hue Hue went on: "Quan, if you really want to know, I'm very scared too—not of the dark, but of loneliness, of being left by myself." "Why don't we move next to each other, then?" asked Quan. "You don't have to feel lonely because I'll be near you and if I feel frightened in the night I can wake you up." They rearranged their sleeping mats alongside one another, the stack of bones between them. The children lay down beside each other and after a long silence they again began to talk—about death.

It was the first time the subject had been mentioned. Calmly Quan said: "You know, Hue Hue, I think I'll be the first to die. But I'm not scared." Hue Hue sat up; there was no doubt in her mind that the little boy was right, but, hoping to encourage him, she said: "No, Quan, I know it's going to be me, and I'm not scared either."

Hue Hue spent the days sitting at her usual place, back against the outer wall of the cabin, forever scanning the sea for a ship and watching for seagulls in the evening. She could no longer catch the smaller birds; they were too clever for her. But, now that there was hardly a sign of human life aboard, the seagulls flew in regularly each evening to roost. When they flighted out in the morning, one of their number was always missing. Weak as she was, Hue Hue's hand had not lost its cunning.

Only once did she falter, and that was about a week after the children had talked about death. That night Hue Hue felt it, too ill to go stalking seagulls. She watched them flight in and land on the stern, counted them, and noted that there was no lack of numbers. Then she went into the cabin and lay down beside Quan. "I'm not feeling well," she said. Quan did not answer; without saying goodnight to each other, they fell asleep.

It was sometime in the middle of the night and very dark when Hue Hue suddenly woke up. Quan was saying something. She listened tensely and heard him murmur: "Tomorrow, Hue Hue, you'll be all right. You'll be able to catch a bird." Hue Hue heard no more and fell asleep.

When she next woke up, the sun was well above the horizon, Quan lay beside her, apparently still asleep. "Wake up, Quan, wake up!" she said, then leaned over toward him. Quan's eyes were still closed, his small, thin face peaceful. Hue Hue felt for his heart; it was no longer beating. His body, though, still felt warm.

Terror seized Hue Hue. She was not surprised that Quan was dead, but now that he was, she was aware of being utterly alone. For some moments she panicked, crying hysterically; then she pulled herself together. She must do something, exert herself in some way, or else she would go out of her mind.

With a hand around each of his wrists she began to pull the dead boy out of the cabin, taking care not to disturb the stack of bones. Though Quan's small body, like her own, weighed almost nothing, Hue Hue was put to the limit of what little strength remained to her to drag it out. With frequent stops to rest, she at last reached the side, and maneuvered the corpse so that on its own it slid away out of sight.

15

Hue Hue made her way back to her place outside the cabin, sat down, and propped herself against the wall. She shut her eyes and her mind filled again with dark, terrifying thoughts. Not a single being remained alive in the whole ship; not one dying with delirious cries breaking the silence; nor even one dead, but tangible, visible, whose body had to be dragged to the side and thrown overboard. As far as she could see there were no more bodies, alive or dead; not a sign of human life. Her eyes shut, Hue Hue could hear only the sea crashing against the wreck, the wind as it whined in the radio antenna at the masthead, and the cry of seagulls wheeling above, as if mocking her.

For a long while she prayed, trying to recover some balance in her mind, to steady her thoughts and emotions and restore her belief in a ship that would come and save her. Then, feeling she had regained possession of herself, she got up and began to go about the various chores that for more than four months she had performed daily on Ladd Reef. She lowered a plastic bucket over the side and drew up seawater, half a bucketful at a time. Too weak to lift the bucket above her head and rinse herself, she stripped and, as best she could, emptied the water over herself, bathing the sores on her arms and dabbing water copiously over her head. Hue Hue's hair, once shiny black, had not been cut for months. The sun and salt air had dried and discolored it so that now it hung, limp and dirty brown, down to her shoulders. It was full of lice, the common affliction of all who were aboard the white ship. The others were now free of the torture, but Hue Hue was nearly driven mad by the itching of her scalp.

Her clothes, already well worn at the start of her ill-fated journey, were in rags. Despite the feebleness in her arms and fingers, she did all she could to rub and rinse out the filth in the bucket of seawater. Then she laid the garments out to dry. Finally Hue Hue swept her cabin clean, then took up her customary station outside the cabin door, waiting, searching for a ship, willing it with all her mind to come sailing by, praying. Day after day she waited, praying when her nerves felt as if they would crack, her prayers now more of an argument than a plea. "You know, Lord Buddha, I can't endure this endless waiting much longer. I'm impatient for a ship to come, but if you don't want to send it, then believe me, I'm equally impatient to die. Send a boat quickly, please, or let me die quickly. One or the other, I really don't mind, but quickly. Don't think I've given up hope; except that now I hope for death as much as I do for life." Hue Hue had not the least intention of lying down and dying. She would make every effort possible to keep alive, to survive. But, oh, God! how often she felt she wanted to die.

As the sun rode down toward the horizon, setting the sea ablaze, and the gigantic balloons of cloud floated higher and higher into the cool, blue-green sky, Hue Hue always felt more at peace. In the depths of her young heart, her body too, she felt a certainty that between the sky and the sea and her there was a liaison of some kind. Minuscule as she was in all that immensity, that eternity of sea and sky, she knew that she was part of it.

She felt the same about her relationship with the seagulls now flighting in to roost. The hunter and the hunted: the association, already close, becomes profoundly intimate when the prey must die to give life to the one who seeks to kill it. Hue Hue, dying, felt part of those living seagulls. As she crept toward her victim she was aware that her failure to catch it would bring her yet closer to death. Her seagull, dead, gave her a further extension of life.

After marking down the seagull she planned to catch, she would go inside the cabin to gnaw at the one she had dried that morning. Hue Hue would bite into the tough, dry meat that clung obstinately to the bone; once she chipped off part of her front tooth on a bone and told herself to be more careful in the future. Her hunger satisfied, she would wait for dark, with no Cuong or Quan to wake her. Then she would creep out, catch her seagull, and bring it back, squawking and struggling, to the cabin. There was no more string, so she tore off strips of cloth to leash the seagull by the leg until next morning, when she could process it into yet another unappetizing meal. Then she would lie down to sleep. She kept the place where she had lain next to Quan before he died. His vacant sleeping mat and the stack of his father's bones beside her created something of his presence and gave her company. Soon she would fall asleep.

Hue Hue still dreamed incessantly, night after night: always the same dreams of home and the family and her friends. People she knew and loved were coming and going to and from her home. They were sitting at table; the food was good, she could smell it, taste it, and always she ate greedily. It was good to be home again, and Hue Hue was her old happy, energetic, confident self, laughing and, when teased by her father, shyly drawing her pretty head down into the hollow of her left shoulder. She saw herself as attractive, coquettish even. Then, as she awoke, the dream began to melt away. She clung to it, trying to stay asleep, fighting reality; but like a bullet in the heart, it hit her.

For nearly two weeks, since Quan died, Hue Hue had been alone in the white ship. One night at the beginning of February 1979, her dreams had a different ending. They began as usual with visions of home and happiness; the dream faded, but this time Hue Hue did not wake up. Instead, another dream began. Cuong and Quan were there, still looking thin and deathly pale as they had been when they died. They were speaking to her—in unison, it seemed—and she heard them quite clearly saying: "Don't worry, Hue Hue, hold on and perhaps tomorrow a boat will come." Then they vanished. Hue Hue woke up and rubbed her eyes.

It was already light, so she got up and, as she did every morning, made her way across to the open cabin door. Before she reached it, she was conscious that somewhere a motor was running. From the cabin door she looked out and there, fifty yards away, was a boat. Beyond it, farther from the shore, there was another.

For an instant, Hue Hue stood looking toward the sea, unable to believe that what she saw was real; a boat, a wooden fishing boat, a few yards away, beyond the stern of the white ship. She felt as if a powerful electric current had been switched on inside her. She picked up a white shirt that had once belonged to Quan and stumbled across the deck toward the stern. She felt as if she were running as fast as she ever had in the races at school. Hardly able to stand, she held onto the side as she waved the shirt, calling over and over again in a husky voice, *"Cun toi voi, cun toi voi!* Help me, help me!"

She could see three men in the boat. They waved back briefly as if to say, "All right, take your time," then fell to discussing something. A few moments later the *banca,* a skiff trailing behind the boat, was pulled alongside. Two men got into it and started paddling toward the white ship. They appeared at the top of the ladder; then, without noticing Hue Hue as she stood by her cabin door, turned and walked toward the stern. From there they turned back and walked toward her, two young men in shirt and shorts, taller than the average South Vietnamese and darker-skinned—more like North Vietnamese. Hue Hue froze with fear as a thought struck her. She had no idea where she was—still not far, perhaps, from the coast of Vietnam. The men might be Vietnamese Communists. If so, they would probably kill her. Hue Hue was so frightened that she began to tremble.

16

Mangsee Great Reef, one of the more than seven thousand islands of the Philippines Republic, is peopled by a community of some three thousand fisherfolk, all of them Muslims. They are refugees from Tawitawi, their former island home two hundred miles to the southwest, where, unwilling to get involved in the insurrections that for some time have plagued the republic, they petitioned the government to move them to a safer, quieter place. That is how they came to be on Mangsee Great Reef, living happily but not all that easily by fishing and diving for shellfish, Chinese clams, and other seafood.

At Mangsee the houses crowd under palm trees, around the white sandy beach and right down on to it—wooden houses on stout bamboo poles and thatched with palm leaves. Beneath them, ducks shelter comfortably from the crushing heat. The mayor, Hadji Hussein, is one of the few who lives in a two-room house of solid bricks and mortar with an airy terrace giving on to a private shipyard. There, with a practiced eye and hand and infinite patience, the local model of fishing boat is built. It is called the *kumpit* and is powered with a Japanese 22 horsepower Yanma diesel engine. Some sixty-five feet long and thirteen in the beam, its smooth, flowing lines are a harmony of clean and complex curves. Each plank of the hull is chipped to size with a light axe until it fits perfectly flush against its neighbor.

One of the *kumpits* of the Mangsee fishing fleet was the motor vessel *Sittirazma*. Its skipper, or patron as they called him, was twenty-eight-year-old Mucktal Hadji Kamaruddin. When not at sea Mucktal was a teacher; fishing and diving for shells in the South China Sea, particularly for a family man like Mucktal, was a hard life, its rewards uncertain. At the end of December, with the worst of the typhoon season over and the monsoon easing somewhat, Mucktal met with his fourteen crewmen to discuss the next fishing trip. The men included his two brothers Hadji Nasser and Kadrie; the remainder were all relations or friends of the family. It was Mucktal himself who suggested that this time they should venture as far as Ladd Reef, 420 nautical miles to the west of Mangsee. Mucktal had talked with the patrons of one or two other *kumpits* who had already been there; they had told him that since the reef was so remote, the fishing, and particularly the shell-diving, were exceptional.

Mucktal's crew were not enthusiastic; the reef was too far away, they protested; but Mucktal insisted. He laid out his chart, a tattered, well-thumbed copy of British Admiralty chart 2660 B, its folds stuck together with Scotch tape, and put his finger on Ladd Reef. "That's where we're going boys," he said, running his finger westward across the chart. "I figure that, fishing and diving as we go, it will take us up to thirty days to get to the London Reefs. We'll stay around as long as there aren't too many other boats around. Then on to Ladd Reef and *in'ch'allah* (God's will be done)."

Mucktal was an excellent patron, they all knew. Within a few days fuel and supplies were stowed aboard; the engine, compass, and tackle were all checked, and the *Sittirazma* was ready to sail.

Friday, January 5, 1979, was the Muslim sabbath. Mucktal and his family prayed in the green-roofed mosque built by the villagers. Next day just before sunrise, he took leave of them in his wooden house by the seashore and walked down to the water's edge where the rest of the crew were gathering. With two or three others he climbed into a *banca*, which was paddled out to the *Sittirazma*, moored in deeper water beyond the end of the wooden jetty. Three other *kumpits* were anchored nearby; all of them, Mucktal knew, were bound eventually for Ladd Reef, but he was determined to be there first.

Shortly after sunrise the *Sittirazma*'s engine was started up and ten minutes later she was under weigh, on a head of 300 degrees, to Commodore Reef. There Mucktal's men got down to work, sometimes trawling for fish but more often diving for shellfish and clams. Using only the power of their lungs and a locally made mask to protect their eyes, the best of them would stay under for two minutes or more at a time. For some days they searched the ocean bed for the bizarre and beautiful shells that would be sold, at exorbitant prices, to tourists in the boutiques of Manila—of New York, Paris, and London, too, perhaps. Then they sailed on, another forty-five sea miles or so, southwest by west to Investigator Shoal; a few more days there, and they were bound northwest on a longish haul to Cornwallis Reef.

Leaving Cornwallis, the *Sittirazma* ran into foul weather and had to reduce speed. The rough sea made diving difficult off Alison, Pearson, and Cuarteron reefs, their next stops. Thanks to the weather, Mucktal lost three days sailing; when the *Sittirazma* at last reached the easternmost of the London Reefs, Mucktal was dismayed to find that the three other Mangsee boats were already there, anchored close to one another. He hailed one of them: "Have you been to Ladd

132

Reef?" "Of course," the man shouted back, laughing. "Where've you been all this time?" Mucktal was not taken in, but he was disappointed. He had meant to spend a few days at the London Reefs, but with the opposition installed before him, he decided to push on that evening. The race was on; but as far as he could see, there was only one serious challenger, who had weighed anchor some moments after the *Sittirazma*.

With daylight next morning, Ladd Reef was in sight. The other *kumpit*, not far astern, was veering toward the west side of the reef while Mucktal kept straight ahead toward the east side. Doubtless, he thought to himself, we shall meet around on the other side. He stopped the *Sittirazma*'s motor off the northeast tip. It was about eight o'clock and already the day was warming up, with a clear sky, not a breath of wind, and a calm sea.

Mucktal praised Allah for such perfect conditions and put twelve men over the side to dive. "I'll keep Kadrie and Omerto with me and take a look around the reef," he told them. "We'll be back in a couple of hours or so." With the *Sittirazma*'s engine idling, Mucktal began to work slowly around to the south side of the reef, toward one of the three wrecks marked on his chart.

Beyond it, some way off shore as he had expected, lay the other *kumpit*. Mucktal steered the *Sittirazma* closer to the wreck, which was so eaten with rust that he could distinguish no name on it. As he passed some twenty yards away from the stern, seagulls rose screaming from the wreck and flew off, and Mucktal was surprised when a figure appeared and waved something white. He just had time to wave back before the figure disappeared. Mucktal called, "Kadrie! There's a man aboard the wreck. Must be from the other *kumpit*. You and Omerto get into the *banca* and go and ask him if they'll sell us a sack of rice. We're nearly out."

The two men climbed into the *banca* and paddled the few yards to the coral, beaching it beside the wreck on the port side. They got out, Kadrie leading. He took hold of the rope extension hanging from the rusted iron ladder fixed to the side of the wreck and began climbing. As ne neared the top he stopped, turned his head, and shouted down to Omerto: "Can you smell it? The stench. It's awful. I can hardly go on." Holding his hand over his face, he stepped aboard, followed by Omerto, who, mouthing a few rude expletives, did the same. The two men walked a few paces toward the stern, past two or three skeletons, which they briefly inspected. Near one of them lay a wallet, which Kadrie, without opening it, shoved into his hip pocket. Then they turned and walked toward the forepart of the ship, passing a grotesque object: the torso of a man, still intact and clothed in a shirt, leaned over the railing of the hold; his legs, decomposed, were those of a skeleton. In disgust, Kadrie and Omerto turned aside, then suddenly stopped short.

A few paces away, leaning against a door beneath the forecastle, there stood a hideous apparition, resembling a small and very old woman, barefoot and dressed in tattered black trousers and a ragged short-sleeved blouse from which hung two arms, bones covered with skin raw with festering sores. Two eyes stared out from hollows sunk into the small face, deeply lined and burned almost black by the sun and half-hidden by dirty, sun-bleached hair that hung down below the shoulder. It was Hue Hue. She was trembling violently. Slowly she raised an emaciated arm, beckoned to the men, and in a coarse whisper said, *"Toi la nguoi Vietnam,* I am from Vietnam." The men caught only one word: "Vietnam." They replied in broken English, their lingua franca, "We Filipino."

17

It was February 3, or thereabouts. Tinh and his family, who had arrived at Ca Mau six weeks before, were still there. Neither he nor Le Mai now believed it possible that Trung and Hue Hue could still be alive; yet, because there was no news, they still kept hoping. They no longer talked of them, however, because the mention of their names made Quang and To cry. The postponement of the MH0126's departure caused Tinh and the four hundred other passengers more irritation than anxiety. They were still in the care of the Ca Mau police and had nothing to worry about—except the events that were happening far from Ca Mau. These were the reasons for the delay in sailing.

In November 1978 Vietnam had signed a treaty of friendship and cooperation with the USSR. The following month, Vietnam invaded China's protégé, Kampuchea. In January 1979 Vietnamese forces occupied the capital Phnom Penh and the Chinese-backed Pol Pot regime was replaced by one headed by Heng Samrin, a friend of Hanoi. In February, China, in order to "teach a lesson" to its unruly neighbor, invaded Vietnam's northern provinces. During the period of hostilities, the ships of Vietnam's new ally, Soviet Russia, plied the coastal waters, taking arms and supplies to Hanoi. The Ca Mau police, loyal to their MH0126 clientele and loath to risk their interception by a Soviet ship and return in captivity to Vietnam, preferred to submit them to the inconvenience of waiting till the coast was clear.

During that tiresome wait at Ca Mau, the police remained on excellent terms with the boat people. Tinh himself invited them regularly to drink a beer or two with him and other friends, and occasionally they spent an evening dining pleasantly, if somewhat sparingly, in a local restaurant. With the police there were no problems.

On the family side, affairs were more difficult. Quang and To, with no school or anything else to keep them occupied, became restless, wondering why they were stuck in Ca Mau, so far from their home and their friends. An occasional visit from one or another of their grandmothers (on the usual pretext of buying rice) helped to restore the situation, but at the beginning of February, with Tet due on the twelfth, Tinh and Le Mai agreed that she should return to Cantho with the boys to spend the festival with their grandmothers. For Tinh there was no question of leaving Ca Mau; he had no intention of once more missing the boat. He would wait there in case the police gave the green light. They were all sad, for the family had never before been separated at Tet. Now Le Mai and the boys were at Cantho, Tinh at Ca Mau, Hue Hue and Trung, they knew not where. Probably dead.

Hue Hue found herself at Cornwallis Reef, feting the full moon, if not Tet, on February 12. She still could hardly believe all that had happened in the last week or so. The moment she had decided to risk a few words in Vietnamese to those two swarthy strangers who had climbed aboard the white ship, and had heard them say the word "Filipino," everything had changed. She had continued to tremble, no longer with fear but with sheer excitement at being safe, rescued at last.

The two men had been kind to her. They were curious to take a look inside her cabin and she too had a final glance around this little triangular hell, which had been her prison for four months and where people—she could not remember how many—had lived and died beside her. There, still, was the little stack of Minh Hung's bones that his boy Quan had cherished, lying beside his sleeping mat and hers. There, too, were the yellow plastic containers used for rainwater, the big knife and a couple of smaller ones with which she and the boys had gutted the seagulls and cut them up. And there, alive and tied to a nail by a strip of cloth attached to its leg, was the seagull she had caught last night. It had been an easy captive for her; for the seagull it would be a reprieve. Hue Hue freed its wings, ripped the cloth strip from its anchorage. But before she could untie the cloth from its leg, the seagull struggled free, and flew off trailing the cloth strip behind it.

Kadrie made as if to pick up Hue Hue and carry her, but she insisted on walking to the top of the ladder. Omerto was waiting below as, very slowly, with Kadrie steadying her, she began to climb down. It was difficult, much more so than the last time over a month ago, when with Mai and Tai they had tried to get to the black ship. Kadrie lifted her—she felt as light as cotton—into the *banca*. A few minutes later, Mucktal and the two others were helping Hue Hue aboard the *Sittirazma*. They put a plate of hot food in front of her—the cooked meat of the shells they had found, and rice cooked in sugar. For months—nearly five months—Hue Hue had never tasted anything so good. They offered her cassava, tapioca, but she found it tasteless. "Eat very slowly," Mucktal explained by signs, "and not too much." It was wise advice, but unnecessary; Hue Hue's stomach simply could not take much.

Mucktal opened up the engine, and the *Sittirazma* gathered way. Hue Hue stopped eating and gazed at the rusted hulk of the white ship. She could not yet take in the events of the last few hours; the dream, the boat, and these kind Filipino fishermen who had saved her from death. It was hard to believe that all the misery and squalor, the ghoulishness, the loneliness, was now behind her. Hue Hue turned her gaze away from the white ship and did not look back again. Before going back to her food, though, she said a silent, fervent prayer: "Thank you, God, for listening to me."

As they passed the other *kumpit*, Mucktal hailed the patron and in a few shouted words told him that he had on board a survivor from the wreck. They rounded the west side of the reef, and Hue Hue gestured to Mucktal to steer as close as possible to the wreck of the black ship. The number of desperate attempts the boat people had made to reach it! Had they succeeded they, or some of them, might have been saved earlier. Trung might have been saved. Hue Hue put the thought out of her mind. What had been, had been. The black ship was a dead ship—witness the flush of seagulls as the *kumpit* approached and the two crumpled skeletons on the coral nearby.

On the northeast corner of Ladd Reef, they passed another wreck, a recent one, to judge by its bright paint. Near it Mucktal beached the *Sittirazma* in order to pick up his twelve divers. They climbed aboard with their haul, a big one, which would help to make up for the bad diving conditions on the way out to Ladd Reef. But still, to cover his outlay and make a profit he would have to make his way back from reef to reef, diving as he had done on the outward voyage. That might take another three weeks.

To his astonished men, Mucktal presented the hideous little scarecrow that was poor Hue Hue, clumsily pronouncing her name. Then the motor was restarted and the *Sittirazma* headed northeast back to the London Reefs. As Hue Hue watched Ladd Reef fall farther and farther behind, she made another silent prayer: "Thank you, Lord Buddha, with all my heart, thank you. I promise you that when I get the chance I'll make you an offering. And when I find my parents we'll all make you a big one of chicken, which I know you like." Suddenly Trung came back into Hue Hue's mind. Chicken was his favorite dish too. Deliberately she put away the thought of him and of her parents too. She was safe, but still she could not realize it. It would need time to sink in. When it had, her parents and brothers would be at the top of her list of things to think about. She would find them; but one thing at a time.

The last time Hue Hue had looked at herself, she had been a plump, pretty schoolgirl. By signs she asked Mucktal for a mirror; the face she saw in it frightened her. Apart from her weakness and her wasted body, Hue Hue suffered from two acutely painful afflictions: sores on her arms and lice in her hair. Mucktal had antiseptics and ointment for her arms; the bare, sticky flesh might take some time to heal, but it should present no problem. Lice were another matter. With more signs she tried to explain to Mucktal: "All on the wreck had lice. We could do nothing about it." Her head was so thick with lice that she could feel them and their eggs with the tips of her fingers. Several showers a day cleared her scalp of the lice and relieved the itching that had tortured her for weeks; but the nits still clung to her hair. Another person was needed for the job of picking them out. Normally it would have been done by a woman, but since there were none aboard, a young member of the crew, Jaynar Eben, took on the unenviable job.

Meanwhile Mucktal told Hue Hue he was sorry, but he

would have to isolate her in the stern. It would be uncomfortable for her, with the noise and fumes of the Yanma diesel, but lice could be a carrier of typhus and other diseases, and he could not afford to risk his crew being infected. When they reached the London Reefs, Mucktal beached the *Sittirazma* on the Sand Patch that forms part of the West Reef. There, day after day, while the rest of the crew were diving or looking for firewood, Jaynar sat beside Hue Hue on the sand, performing his delicate task. After the session was over, there remained another exercise, equally important. Hue Hue now had to learn to walk properly. After three days she could cover the two hundred yards of the sand patch, though her back muscles were still so weak that she walked with a stoop. At the end of the day she was helped back to the *kumpit* to spend the night. Mucktal and his men, superstitious sailors, felt more secure aboard; Hue Hue too.

Next morning Mucktal left the West Reef, steered clear of the Central Reef, where, fishermen's hearsay had it, a Taiwanese garrison was stationed, and came to the Cuarteron Reef. There he ran into more Taiwanese—fishermen this time. Between fishermen in these waters there exists a code of mutual respect; with the military they never knew what to expect. The stay at Cuarteron turned into something of a fete for Hue Hue. She and the Taiwanese talked away in their own lingua franca, Mandarin. They made much of her, invited her to eat with them, and offered to take her back to Taiwan and from there send a cable to her parents.

Hue Hue asked the fishermen: "Would you just send a cable for me when you return?" They replied, rather unkindly, that they would do so only if she would accompany them. On this tiny reef in the middle of the Chinese sea, Hue Hue found herself in a dilemma. She remembered her father saying that he would never resettle in another Asian country because all of them, he feared, would one day be Communist. Thanking the Taiwanese fishermen, Hue Hue told them; "I'm sorry, I can't go with you." So they sent her back to the *Sittirazma* with a bottle of soy sauce and some shampoo, made in Taiwan, green and guaranteed to lather in seawater. For Mucktal they sent a bag of flour.

At Pearson Reef the *Sittirazma* anchored at the west end of the reef. Mucktal had misgivings about the Vietnamese garrison that he knew to be stationed at the eastern extremity, and Hue Hue was still more disturbed when he told her about them. She grimaced and drew her hand across her throat as a sign that if they caught her, they would kill her. The wreck of a large Chinese junk lay close by the spot where they had anchored; Hue Hue spent an hour slowly pacing its deck, which was much easier than stumbling over the rough coral. *Sittirazma*'s company spent an uneasy night on account of the Vietnamese garrison and were glad to move on next day to Alison Reef.

It was February 12 when they came to the Cornwallis Reef. As the full moon rose that night, laying a silver path from the horizon up to the *Sittirazma*, where Hue Hue sat on deck with the sailors, it did not strike her that it was the first night of Tet, the Chinese new year. She had lost all notion of time, at least of time recorded by the calendar.

Since leaving Ladd Reef, the fishermen had made her learn a few words of their Filipino Tagalog and she in return had taught them some Mandarin words. The fishermen were always humming or singing as they went about their jobs. They had asked Hue Hue to sing for them, but she made them understand that her voice was too weak. That night, however, they all gathered on deck beneath the full moon with Hue

Hue in their midst and sang song after song, and Hue Hue, carried away in the atmosphere of moonlight and song, felt enough courage to reply. She sang for them, "A Beautiful Sunday"—in Mandarin—and repeated it, helping them to follow the words. Then the fishermen sang back to her, "Darling, darling," in English, with Hue Hue doing her best to imitate them. Among those fifteen brawny men, Hue Hue felt happy; yet when she thought of her family, she realized it was a fleeting sort of happiness and that the sentimental, singsong atmosphere made her long to be with them.

That same evening, four hundred miles away across the South China Sea at Ca Mau, Hue Hue's father was celebrating Tet, somewhat reluctantly, with a few Communist police officers; at Cantho, Le Mai and the little boys were spending a cozy evening with their adoring grandmothers.

18

From the Cornwallis Reef it was a long haul southeast to the Investigator Shoal, and by the time the *Sittirazma* had anchored there, Hue Hue was beginning to fret. She signed to Mucktal to show her the chart and to tell her where they were going and—with a desperate gesture—how much longer it would take. Mucktal put his finger on Investigator Shoal. Then he ran it across to Commodore Reef not far away, and down to Mangsee, a good deal farther. He counted on his fingers: one, two, three. Three days more to Mangsee.

Mucktal was in a dilemma. He had to go on diving and fishing and complete his voyage as planned, otherwise he would never recover his outlay, let alone make a profit. No one was likely to compensate him if he failed to do so. Yet he was well aware that he should get the little girl back to land and proper medical care as quickly as possible.

Since they had rescued Hue Hue from Ladd Reef about two weeks ago, she and the fishermen had each understood little of what the other was trying to say. She did understand, however, that they were superstitious about ghosts and evil spirits. She had managed to convey to them that, while Ladd Reef was naturally haunted by the spirits of the poor boat people who had died there, she herself did not fear them, because her father had always told her not to. They believed her. But Mucktal now noticed that Hue Hue was not so sure of herself. Since leaving Pearson Reef he had kept her on board, believing that she was afraid to go ashore. That might have been so; the horrors of Ladd Reef and the white ship were perhaps catching up with her. If they were, Hue Hue never admitted as much. It could have been just that she was not interested in anything but getting to Mangsee. Mucktal realized that the sooner he got back there, the better. Mangsee, however, proud as it was of its mosque, boasted no such thing as a hospital. The nearest one was still nearly a week's voyage away, at Puerto Princesa, Palawan Island.

It was around 4 P.M. on February 19 when the *Sittirazma* tied up to the end of the rough wooden jetty at Mangsee. To avoid the rough-hewn wide-spaced planks of the jetty, Mucktal helped Hue Hue into a *banca* and with his two brothers paddled it through the clear shallow water to the shore. Mucktal and his crew were in good spirits; they had brought back a big haul of fish and shells as well as the young survivor from Ladd Reef. The other *kumpits* that had been to the reef had already returned and spread the word. The whole of Mangsee, a chattering crowd in brightly colored shirts and sarongs, flocked down to the beach to welcome the *Sittirazma*.

The Barangay chairman, Hadji Hussein, more formally dressed than usual in blue blazer and beige trousers with a white turban wrapped about his head, was the first to welcome Mucktal and his men; then Hue Hue was presented to him. For Hadji Hussein and the citizens of Mangsee it was a moving occasion. Neither he nor they had forgotten that they were once refugees from oppression in Tawitawi and that in Mangsee they had once more found freedom, within the law,

144

to do and think as they pleased. Hadji had a soft spot for refugees, especially the boat people; Mangsee fishermen had already rescued some thirty of them and brought them ashore.

So dense was the throng around Hue Hue's *banca* that, to get a better view, some villagers climbed onto the roofs of nearby houses. One caved in, badly hurting three people. In Mangsee today, everyone, including those who were small children at the time, will tell the visitor: "Yes, we remember Hue Hue. We shall never forget her." They will say, "*Makasis*, she was pitiful," and "*Massi, massi*, we felt so sorry for her." Others will murmur, "*Vasali, vasali*, we feel the same." And then they will all chorus, "We want Hue Hue to come back." Those warmhearted fisherfolk wanted Hue Hue to stay with them. Mucktal's elder brother Hadji Nasser, a man of influence in the community, told Hue Hue he would like to adopt her; his wife readily agreed. She would accept Hue Hue as her own daughter. They took her into their house, fed her—with fish, again—and fussed over her. She spent the night with them, but even as she lay wondering at the generosity of these people, the thought of staying among them did not occur to her. She must find her parents and her brothers. How or where she had no idea, but find them she would.

Hue Hue was to be plied with many and various kindnesses, with gifts and offers of sponsorship and adoption. These often tempted her, but she obstinately refused to be deflected from her prime object: to find her parents. She remembered her father saying many times that he was determined at all costs to escape from Vietnam. She was sure he would have done so by now and wherever in the world he might be, she was resolved to find him.

Early next morning a Filipino navy patrol vessel anchored

off Mangsee and a small party of officials and khaki-clad marines came ashore. Hadji Hussein and Mucktal escorted them to the house of Hadji Nasser, where they had talked for a while. When they finished, Mucktal made Hue Hue understand that she was being taken to the military hospital at Puerto Princesa. He and his brother were sad to lose her, Mucktal explained, but he realized it would be best for her. At the foot of the wooden ladder leading down from the house to the sand, she said good-bye to Hadji Nasser's wife. Then with him and Mucktal she walked toward the *banca* through the crowd, as big as yesterday's, who were begging her, "Stay with us, Hue Hue." Hue Hue thought, "In a way I'd like to, they're so kind," but her eyes were fixed on the *banca* and beyond it the patrol vessel. She was about to resume the journey that, God willing, would take her back to her family.

At the *banca* she stopped and in Cantonese, mixed with some Tagalog words she had picked up from Mucktal, she said good-bye to him and Hadji Nasser. Nasser pressed three notes of a hundred pesos into her hand, saying, "Keep them, buy yourself something." There were tears in Hue Hue's eyes as she repeated once more the Tagalog phrase she knew best: "*Maraming salamat*, thank you very much." From the *banca*, as it moved away, Hue Hue waved to the brothers and the crowd around them who kept calling, "Hue Hue, come back!" Then Filipino sailors helped her aboard the patrol vessel, which headed northward across the Balabac Strait. Hue Hue's quest for her parents had begun in earnest.

A long and tedious voyage lay ahead. That evening, they reached the small naval harbor of Balabac, surrounded by steep wooded hills. There Hue Hue spent three uncomfortable days and nights, torn between the sympathy everyone showed her and her impatient longing to be on her way. The patrol boat left again at last, heading northeast in the lee of the hilly coastline of the southern tip of Palawan Island. Two days later it docked at Brookes Point, and from there Hue Hue was driven in an army truck the nine miles to the grass airstrip at San Marinana, headquarters of the 2nd Marine Brigade. The commander, Colonel Rodolfo Biazon, a tall, kindly man, immediately had her brought a copious plate of rice and vegetables, which she devoured, as she did a similar plate, three hours later, when she lunched with the colonel.

Rodolfo Biazon was struck by Hue Hue's intelligence, the still very evident marks of malnutrition, and her voracious appetite. Another thing that struck the colonel was that poor Hue Hue was continually scratching at her head; neither the efforts of Jaynar nor the green shampoo from Taiwan had yet succeeded in ridding it of lice. She spoke to Colonel Biazon of "mama" and "papa" and her two young brothers. They might still be in Vietnam, but even if they were, she was sure they would leave one day; no matter what, she would find them.

Rodolfo Biazon led her out to the waiting aircraft, an old de Havilland Beaver that had seen better days but still flew like a bird. She gave him a big smile and shook his hand, then climbed up the few steps in the side of the aircraft and sat down behind the pilot. It was the first time Hue Hue had flown, but she felt no special thrill. Her mind was on other things. She was pleasantly aware that she was feeling better. Her appetite, she realized, was returning with a vengeance and she smiled when she thought of the way she had downed those two enormous plates of rice. She recalled what she had told the colonel about her parents and brothers and, for the first time, the conviction came to her that she would find them again. Then she fell asleep.

When an hour or so later the Beaver landed at Puerto

Princesa, Hue Hue was led to the waiting room. After a while a man entered and said to her, smilingly, in Vietnamese: "*Cung toi day lan chua?* Have you been waiting long, my dear?" It was Van Danh Bao, the chairman of the U5 Vietnamese Refugee Camp. To her embarrassment, Hue Hue at first found herself tongue-tied, unable to find the Vietnamese words to reply; for five months, living with the Cantho group aboard the white ship, she had spoken only Cantonese.

Van Danh Bao took Hue Hue to be registered at the refugee camp down by the sea, just beyond the end of the airport runway. With others, she was squatting in front of the administrative building waiting her turn, when something made her look up. To her astonishment, she found herself staring straight into the face of her schoolteacher, Huynh My. Hue Hue stood up, and the two greeted each other politely. Neither had ever felt much sympathy for the other, and Hue Hue wondered what unfortunate coincidence had brought them both from the Tho Nhon High School in Cantho, by different ways, to meet a thousand miles away, in Palawan.

After she had registered her name and the date, February 25, Hue Hue went by military jeep to the hospital. She thought no more, for the time being, about Huynh My.

The headquarters of the Philippines Western Command— WESCOM—are a few miles up the dusty red-earth road from the refugee camp. The drooping fronds of coconut palms give shade to the buildings and access roads. One road leads down to the shore and a row of wooden bungalows, their airy terraces looking straight out onto a narrow beach beyond which mango saplings protrude here and there from the shallow inshore water. In one of the bungalows lived WESCOM's commander in chief, Commodore Gil Fernandez, a bon vivant whose ebullient nature was matched by his apparently inexhaustible energy. The commodore's command included

Palawan Island and extended east and south over the Sulu Sea and west across the South China Sea and its hundreds of reefs and islets, many of them disputed among the Philippines, Taiwan, and Vietnam. The western limit of this vast area of sea was a line running southwest from the North Danger group to Jubilee Bank, hard by Ladd Reef. That is why WESCOM officials, headed by Colonel Igualdad Cunanan, and marines had turned up at Mangsee the day after Hue Hue's arrival. They were the commodore's men. Now that Hue Hue had arrived at the commodore's headquarters, he gave orders to his chief medical officer, Colonel Hugo Javier, a veteran in tropical medicine, to take special care of his patient, to spoil her as much as he wanted, and nurse her quickly back to health.

At nine o'clock the day following her arrival, the doctor made a superficial examination of Hue Hue. Without an interpreter, they had a problem of communication, but despite it the doctor found that, mentally, his patient was surprisingly alert and composed, save that she still grieved deeply for her brother. As for her severe sunburn, the scars on her arms, and the lice in her hair, Dr. Javier had no worries; time and the proper medicines would soon put them right. He prescribed no special treatment for Hue Hue, other than care and kindness and, apart from her normal meals, jam and crackers for tea. That phenomenally tough little girl should, in the doctor's view, make a complete recovery.

Soon after Hue Hue's arrival at the hospital, news of her exploit leaked out. She quickly became a sensation in the international press. Local and national newspapers in places as far apart as London, Louisiana, Malaysia, and Sydney carried headlines such as GIRL'S HORROR-BOAT ESCAPE; BOAT GIRL STILL TREMBLES FROM HER HORROR AT SEA. The stories written about her or supposedly written by her did not always show much regard for the facts. She was featured worldwide as learning for the first time to brush her teeth, though she had done so since she could remember with her favorite Vietnamese toothpaste, Hynos. A lengthy story about her experience was said to have been written by Hue Hue herself. When asked about it, she firmly denied having written anything for the press. Her comment on the presumed author was "A very bad person." The truest words about Hue Hue came from the Australian Minister for Immigration, who declared: "That some like this young girl should be forced to undergo an ordeal that no human should be asked to endure underlines the contempt for the human rights of their own citizens being displayed by the governments of Indochina."

Hue Hue's story and the reports about her, incomplete or inaccurate as they were, helped to focus world attention on the tragedy of the boat people. They also brought many enthusiastic offers from the world over from kind people anxious to sponsor, protect, or adopt Hue Hue. Dr. Javier himself, moved by the ordeal of the girl and her extraordinary fortitude, asked her: "Will you allow me to adopt you, to make you part of my family, along with my other daughters?" He had been so kind to Hue Hue she did not want to hurt him by saying flatly no. But inside herself she knew she could not agree to be adopted by him or anyone else. She must and she would rejoin her parents, wherever they were. As far as she knew, they were still in Vietnam. She asked for a cable to be sent to her father. It was dated March 1, 1979, and said: *CON DA DEN PHI LUAT TAN BINH AN TAT CA NHUNG NQUOI DI CHUNG VOI CON DEU CHET HET*, I have arrived in the Philippines alive and well. Binh, Trung and everybody else dead. Signed, Tran Hue Hue.

The cable never reached Tinh. He, Le Mai, and the two boys had left Ca Mau two days earlier, on February 27.

19

From Tinh's rented house in Ca Mau it was about a hundred yards down to the River Song Doc where the MH0126 was moored. On February 27 word went around among the waiting passengers that the departure was set for nine o'clock that night, well after dark. To make doubly sure that the boarding would be hidden from the prying eyes of the local inhabitants, the police threw a cordon around the area. A captain of the security police came aboard, and the boat cast off; he remained in charge until it reached the Song Doc River police station, the last checkpoint before the estuary. There the police boarded the boat and under the captain's watchful eye began systematically to frisk each passenger, old and young, stripping everyone of gold or money; identity cards were also confiscated. Tinh, before leaving, had heard about this operation; the police with whom he had kept on such good terms had made no secret of it, so he had hidden in the sole of his sandals some of the gold leaf he normally carried in the pockets of his belt. The rest, with some dollar bills, he had rolled neatly inside the cigarettes—in the pack he carried in his trouser pocket. As for Le Mai's gold necklace and the boys' rings, these he carried with a few simple necessities in a plastic bag. The police carefully checked the contents, but without discovering the necklace and rings, which Tinh had sewn into the seams. As he watched the police, Tinh smiled to himself and thought: "This time I've fooled them."

After they had been robbed of the last vestiges of their fortunes, the boat people were treated to a harangue from the police captain. If intercepted by a naval patrol, he advised them, they should say that they were returning to their relatives in China. When they reached Malaysia (where he knew they were going) they were to say nothing against the police, the *bo doi*, or the Vietnamese government. "Always remember your mother country!" he concluded, and Tinh felt quite moved, thinking that if ever by a miracle Vietnam once again got a democratic government, he would certainly go back there. Then the Vietnamese flag, hanging limply at the boat's masthead, was pulled down and carried away by a policeman. With that final act of riddance, the MH0126 moved off downstream into the estuary and onto a southwesterly course, bound for Pulau Bidong Island, Malaysia, the first stop on the journey to exile.

Everything had gone smoothly; the sea was calm. The passengers resigned themselves now to three days and nights of acute discomfort, wedged one against another, sleeping, eating, and doing everything else with an almost complete lack of privacy. They sailed out of the night of the twenty-seventh into the next day and on again into the following night. Then the sea became rougher, and nearly everyone was sick, Tinh and his elder boy Quang included. But not To: Out of pity for his brother, he did not remind him till later that he had won his bet.

Though the boat captain's eyes never left the compass, the boat was nevertheless driven eastward off its course. In the early hours of the morning, as the weather worsened and fear began to creep into the hearts of the refugees, a big oceangoing liner, fully lit up, was sighted overtaking them on a parallel course. The MH0126 fired a distress rocket. Tinh watched it rush upward and break into a red and green flare that came arcing downward through the sky, and he felt certain that the liner's lookout must have seen it. But the big ship sailed on and was lost to sight.

The MH0126 foundered on through the rest of that night and the following day, taking a lot of water over the gunwales, which drenched the people on deck. About midday a cry went up: "Fire!" It was one of the engines, overheating under the strain of the rough sea. Blankets were hung overboard and passed back to men who succeeded, amid clouds of smoke and steam, in damping down the heat. Meanwhile, the engine, throttled down, kept on running.

Next morning, March 2, the captain scanned the horizon ahead through his glasses and then let out an excited shout: "Land Ahoy!" The boat people took up the shout with a clamor of cheers, shrill cries, and moans of relief from those feeling half-dead with seasickness.

The land ahead was not Pulau Bidong, but a small island unidentified on the captain's map, which was no more than a page torn from a school atlas. Toward eleven o'clock the MH0126, with engines idling and the passengers crowded on deck, was approaching the shore, where men of the Malaysian navy waited. One of them signaled to the boat to stop and drop anchor. A sampan carrying a dozen sailors set out from the shore. The sailors, some carrying rifles, other brandishing knives, climbed aboard the boat. Despite their menacing attitude the Malaysian officer in charge, after inspecting the boat, told the captain: "I see many of your people are in a poor way; you may all come ashore." The MH0126 moved alongside the wooden jetty and tied up.

So began a stay of over two weeks on the island. The boat

people slept aboard but went ashore to fetch their daily ration of food—a small cupful of Chinese noodles doled out by the sailors. More could be bought, and Tinh had to sell Le Mai's necklace and the boys' rings in order to raise the money. Even then all he could buy was rice and baked beans. Every day, for sixteen days, they ate baked beans; after that Tinh never wanted to see a baked bean again for the rest of his life.

Fresh water came from a well, the only one on the island. The ration was half a plastic container per family, which came to about a cupful a day for each person. The guard on duty at the well, when the spirit moved him, beat the drawers of water with a stick. Tinh caught several blows; Quang and To, though they dodged, were hit more often. After sixteen days, the well ran dry, and the MH0126 was ordered to move on to Pulau Bidong, an hour's sail away.

Tinh, for one, was glad. For some days, Le Mai had been unusually silent and withdrawn, as if she had something on her mind. Two days before they left the island, she told Tinh what it was: she was expecting a baby.

Both of them were amazed. They loved each other and for the last ten years, since To's arrival, had made love with each other but never with the hope or intention of having another baby. Now that Le Mai was pregnant it seemed to them like a gift from God, a new child to replace at least one of their two missing children. Tinh was at a loss to explain how it could have happened. He was inclined to believe that, because he had helped clean out the temple daily during his stay in Ca Mau, that act of virtue had been rewarded. Tinh and Le Mai, though deeply perplexed, were glad beyond measure.

On March 18 the MH0126 came alongside the jetty at Pulau Bidong. Many more Vietnamese boats, some still intact, some just wooden hulks smashed by the sea, were beached, half buried in the sand or partly awash. Pulau Bidong—Bidong Island—with its steep, densely wooded hills running down into the sea or here and there to a beach fringed with coconut palms, is some four hours' sailing in a local fishing boat from Kuala Trengganu, a small port on Malaysia's east coast. Since July 1978, the island had served as a temporary refuge for boat people for whom Thailand, with its overcrowded refugee camps and coastal waters infested with pirates, had become a less attractive destination than Malaysia. Soon the boat people were overcrowding Malaysia's camps and squatting on its east-coast beaches. The government hoped that Pulau Bidong would relieve the pressure as well as isolate the boat people from the mainland. Hitherto an uninhabited island, it had grown in population to over 45,000 before the end of the year.

The people and notably the fishermen of Malaysia's east-west ports had been sympathetic to the boat people, many of whom they had rescued and given shelter. But as their numbers increased, the government decided to drive the refugees off—at gunpoint—or tow them back to sea. It created a special task force for the purpose and ordered fishermen to be punished for helping them. On a more humane note, it created the refugee camp on Pulau Bidong.

The island refugee camp has usually been described by the media as hell; that is, a hell provided by the Malaysian Red Crescent Society and other voluntary bodies, with funds generously supplied by the UN High Commissioner for Refugees. A hell from which, within a year or so of its opening, some twenty thousand refugees from Communist oppression had been sent on to some democratic country.

Certainly in mid-1979 the main jetty and the nearby "Supply Beach" still smelled like hell because of the mountains of garbage that were partially hidden by the flies that swarmed over them. The housing at Pulau Bidong was fairly hellish, too. There was not a permanent dwelling house on the island, but an agglomeration of bamboo shacks, each one wrapped around with sheets of plastic, white or blue or both, to attempt to keep out the driving tropical rain. The refugees constructed these shacks from bamboo and timber cut from the hillsides, which were now stripped bare.

Tinh was allotted a vacant hut for himself and his family some way up the hill behind the Administrative Building. His hut was not, like those on the flat, wet ground below, perched on poles; it was built foursquare around solid uprights and covered by an iron roof supported on bamboo rafters. A broad bench of bamboo slats served as a bed, with squares of cardboard as mattress. Among the bamboo slums there led narrow, uneven paths, usually slippery with rain and with water from an open drain that ran alongside; where they climbed the hillside the paths sometimes became part of the drainage system, itself a slimy rivulet.

But in this hell were laughing children; children studying in airy classrooms built, like their homes, of bamboo and timber; more children outside playing football with a bundle of newspaper tied with string, or sailing homemade boats in the main drain, or simply running behind the sweating pink-faced visitors from Europe, crying out "Hy'o! How you?" A friendly enough welcome to hell.

On Religion Hill the devout, according to their faith, worshipped in the Buddhist temple, the Roman Catholic Church, or the Reformed church, simple timber buildings that satisfied the boat people's need for prayer. Below, on one side of Religion Hill and overlooking the Supply Beach, two timber-built hospitals, one for the very sick, the other for out-patients, were served by a small but devoted medical staff. On the other side of the Hill, on "Zone C" beach and beside the path leading down to it, merchants and their children squatted next to upturned wooden cases, lit up at night by candles, on which they had laid out their goods—basic things like cakes and Coke and cigarettes, combs, tissues and cheap scent—goods smuggled in by Malay fishermen from the mainland at night, a black-market that the island police regarded with a benevolent if not altogether blind eye. They took the same line about the Pulau Bidong Nightclub and the Lamp Nightclub on the seashore. These establishments catered to an enthusiastic clientele who, despite the prohibition of dancing and alcoholic drinks, seemed to find contentment in the blaring pop music and the classic decor of tall palm trees etched on the moonlit sky.

Pulau Bidong, for the boat-people at least, was not all hell. They had known a worse one in Vietnam. Pulau Bidong was a stopping place, a purgatory perhaps, but on the way to a free country.

The hub of Pulau Bidong's essential activity—the resettlement of refugees—was an open-sided wooden edifice roofed with corrugated iron upon which the tropical rain hammered like machine-gun fire. Called the Administrative Building, it served also as a dormitory. The absence of beds obliged visitors—delegates from "third country" governments and others concerned with the boat people—to sleep on the floor or, if lucky, on a bench or office table, where they were better isolated from the rats that scampered all night long through the building and across the roof. The bathhouse and latrine were a short but muddy walk away.

Food and water were brought in by ship from the mainland and distributed by the Malaysian Red Crescent. Every morning on the Supply Beach, thousands of people congregated to receive the daily handout and to exchange the latest from the grapevine. Every one of the boat people had a story to tell.

Tinh's own story was one among thousands. But it did not end at Pulau Bidong. One morning, a few days after his arrival, Tinh was waiting among the crowd on the supply beach when a man came up to him. He hesitated for a moment, then asked: "You're Luong Tinh, the father of Tran Hue Hue?" "Yes," said Tinh. "I'm Tran Dan," the other went on. "We met once or twice in Cantho. I arrived here not long ago. A few days before I left Cantho, your brother-in-law Hien showed me a telegram he had received at the beginning of March. It was signed Tran Hue Hue. You needn't worry any more, Luong Tinh," he went on. "Your daughter Hue Hue is alive, but everybody else in the boat died. Your son Trung is dead—my young cousin also. He was in the same boat."

"Trung is dead." Tinh, unable to bear the news, broke down and cried. Then, recovering himself, he remembered, "Hue Hue is alive." He could not believe it. How could she have survived and not Trung? At all costs Le Mai must not know; in her present state she would be shattered by the report, which was very likely not even true.

Tinh thanked Tran Dan, collected his stores, and walked up from the beach to the hut of a close friend, Phieu, whose boy also was on Hue Hue's boat. He told him about his conversation with Tran Dan and the gist of the telegram. "Everyone is dead except Hue Hue." Astonished, Phieu asked: "How is it possible that all the passengers, most of them young men like my boy, could be dead while Hue Hue is alive? No, Tinh, don't believe the telegram; it can't be true."

Tinh wondered. He returned to his hut to find Le Mai and the two boys in tears. "Tran Dan has been around," she sobbed. "Thinking I knew he spoke of the telegram, and my heart seemed to stop. So Trung is dead. I believe it now. But I cannot believe that Hue Hue can still be alive." Tinh tried to console her. "I can hardly believe it is true either, but let's keep hoping."

The days that followed were full of anguish and uncertainty for both of them. Tinh wrote to his cousin, Ly To, in Australia. He inquired left and right among his friends: "How can I get more news?" No one could tell him until one morning—nearly three weeks later on April 15—the camp loudspeaker blared: "Anyone wishing for help in contacting relatives or friends abroad, please go to the Malaysian Red Crescent office."

Tinh went straight to his friend Phieu, who could speak English. Some minutes later, in the Red Crescent office, Phieu was drafting a letter in English for Tinh and Le Mai's signatures. It was addressed to the International Red Cross Delegation at Kuala Lumpur, Malaysia's capital, and began with the conventional formula, "We, the undersigned . . ." The letter went on:

> My daughter called Tran Hue Hue . . . escaped from Vietnam on September 13, 1978. Since then we didn't receive any news about her. . . . Two weeks ago one newcomer told us that my relatives in Saigon have received information . . . that she has met an accident on the sea and been saved. Actually she is only one alive and still resting in a military hospital in Philippine (We don't know the name). We would like to know some real information.

A week later, on April 24, Tinh's letter arrived on the desk of Knut Anders in his office at the Red Crescent Tracing and Mail Service in Kuala Lumpur. Anders was doing a spell there as adviser. As he read the letter, his mind went back to a newspaper clipping his wife had sent him from Germany, about a sole survivor. No name was mentioned, but Anders felt sure that it must be the Tran Hue Hue mentioned in Tinh's letter. The Tracing Service went into action.

Meanwhile, the boat people grapevine had also been at work. Two days before Knut Anders received Tinh's letter, the loudspeaker at Pulau Bidong asked Tinh to report personally to the Administrative Building. Tinh, with the two boys, ran down the little path. A telegram was handed to him.

He carefully slit it open and read: "Hue Hue is safe. Don't worry. Am sponsoring her to come to Australia." It was signed Ly To. Hue Hue was alive—it was confirmed by Ly To! Good cousin Ly To. Tinh knew he could trust him.

Tinh did not conceal his joy. He told the boys and, in front of everyone, hugged them while they all repeated, "Hue Hue is alive," and the boys jumped up and down with excitement. Then they ran up the path toward their hut. Before they reached it, they could see Le Mai sitting inside, staring vacantly in their direction. Together they all cried out to her, "Hue Hue's alive!" Le Mai, suddenly galvanized, stood up, ran to meet them, and embraced them one by one. "So Hue Hue at least is alive," she said quietly to Tinh; and she thought, but did not say aloud, "If only Trung were too."

20

In the WESCOM hospital at Palawan, Hue Hue had astonished Dr. Javier by her vitality. Though she was having no special treatment, the doctor had kept her under close observation. After a few days he had gotten to know her better and marveled at the determination and iron constitution that had enabled his young patient to survive the horrible ordeal. Now she was pleading with him to allow her to go and join her own people in the refugee camp, to get "reintegrated."

Before him stood a smiling, scrawny little girl, all bones and joints, her hair thin and lifeless, her skin burnt nearly black by the sun, fresh scars healing all over her arms. The damage, unsightly as it was, was not irreparable. Otherwise, her hair was now free of lice, and, though it was hardly credible, there was nothing wrong with Hue Hue. She would need several more weeks of care and kindness, but this she could best find at the camp among boys and girls of her own age, from her own country. "All right," Dr. Javier told her, "you may go to the camp. Van Danh Bao will let me know if you need anything more from us."

The U5 camp in Puerto Princesa, a flat open space surrounded by a few strands of barbed wire, was situated just beyond the airport runway; but when, morning and afternoon, BAC–111 planes of the domestic airline roared low overhead as they took off for Manila, hardly a refugee looked up. A few trees gave the people who sat chatting beneath them scant shelter from the torrid sun. Girls, prettily dressed in shirts and trousers of printed cotton, drew water out of a hand pump and youths played handball on a well-worn pitch. The U5 camp, where the boat people were counted in hundreds, not thousands as at Pulau Bidong, was run by WESCOM and, for that reason, well run.

The boat people, housed in solid wooden huts, twenty or thirty to a hut, slept in equally solid two-tier iron beds. Opposite the guard room a small bar, which did a lively trade in soft drinks, ice cream, and cigarettes, was also the convenient terminal for the motorcycle taxis that plied between the camp and the town, "Puerto" as it is known. Small cousins of the "Jeepnies" of Manila, they somehow contrived to squeeze four passengers and the driver under a flimsy, fancy-colored canopy and for a price even the destitute boat people could afford.

A bed was found for Hue Hue among the twenty or so others in Bao's hut. Well, here I am, thought Hue Hue, more satisfied with life than she had felt for a long time. But a day or two later her heart sank when her former teacher Huynh My came and said: "You're coming to live in my hut." Hue Hue immediately felt in her tone echoes of the unhappy teacher-pupil relationship of the high school. In her hut down by the seashore, Huynh My allotted the top tier of a bed to her onetime pupil, and from now on made her feel she was back at high school.

Hue Hue prefers not to discuss her relationship with her schoolteacher. All she has to say is: "I'll never forget the way she treated me and the things she said to me. My parents never used such language." Hue Hue, after all she had been through, was badly hurt. But she did not let it worry her too much; Ladd Reef had made her philosophical about suffering, almost immune to it.

Within two weeks Hue Hue had made many friends, who helped her with her work and did their best to give her fun. There was Sergeant Gomez, a tall, tight-lipped and soft-spoken Filipino whose job it was to watch over Hue Hue and report to Dr. Javier if she had any problems. The condition of her hair and skin had improved; the scars on her arms had healed; but she was putting on weight so fast and becoming so plump that she took to doing slimming exercises every evening in the hut. When Sergeant Gomez teased her for being too fat she just laughed. Hue Hue often laughed now, jumping up and down excitedly—as her young brothers Quang and To did at Pulau Bidong when they heard that their sister was still alive.

Hue Hue waited anxiously for an answer to the cable that she had addressed to her father in Cantho. It finally came, but in the form of a cable from the faithful Ly To in Sydney, a repeat of the cable that he had received from Tinh's brother-in-law, Hien, in Cantho: "*Nhhan duoc dien-tie traloi.* Your message safely received." Ly To added: "Please cable your news as soon as possible." But where were her parents? Were they still in Vietnam, or had they escaped? If the latter, no one knew better than Hue Hue the perils of the South China Sea. Ly To's telegram only partly relieved her anxiety.

A few days later, as Hue Hue sat on her bed eating the midday meal of rice and vegetables, someone brought her a letter—a pale blue airmail letter with Ly To's name and address on the back. Hue Hue put down her plate, slit the letter open, and read. Ly To had written: "Your parents and brothers are safe in Malaysia. Do not go away with anyone else, or let yourself be adopted. I am sponsoring your settlement in Australia."

Hue Hue needed a few moments for the message to sink in. Then, under her breath, she gave a tiny exclamation, "Oi!" and got on with her meal. Deep inside herself she experienced a feeling of huge relief. The tremendous news brought Hue Hue a step nearer her family, but she was not there yet. She said to herself, "God will take care of everything," and lost no sleep that night.

Indeed God, through the agency of the UN High Commissioner for Refugees and the Australian Immigration Department in Manila, was taking care of everything. Henceforth Hue Hue would be in their good hands until she was settled in Australia. Hue Hue's immigration to Australia had been approved personally by Michael MacKellar, Minister for Immigration. On May 5, Hue Hue looked down on the U5 camp for the last time as she took off for Manila. There she was lodged in the Army General Hospital at Fort Bonifacio. Her new surroundings overlooked a beautiful park, with purple bougainvillea clambering alongside the road, which led among trees adorning wide swards of well-mown grass, past the golf course and the American Cemetery: a striking change from Palawan, a dramatic one from the dreary inhospitable coral of Ladd Reef.

It was here in a large but overcrowded dormitory that the boat people spent the last days of their stay as guests of the hospitable Filipinos. At the foot of every bed, each with its mosquito net of pink, green, or white, were piled cooking utensils and a heap of miscellaneous baggage. The dormitory floor seethed with children playing cards or table tennis, or simply screaming with joy. In this building Hue Hue spent another three weeks. On May 31 she flew to Sydney, Australia.

The media had not forgotten Hue Hue. At Kingsford Smith Airport in Sydney, she found herself confronted by a crowd of international television, radio, and newspaper reporters. Bewildered by the glare of their spotlights and blinding flashbulbs, confused by their barrage of questions, she faced them, unsmilingly, for twenty minutes. Then she was driven to the government hostel for Vietnamese refugees near East Hills, a pretty western suburb, where Ly To was waiting for her. When her family arrived—soon, she hoped—they would all move into an apartment in the hostel.

Meanwhile the Immigration Department had arranged for her to stay at Revesby, close to East Hills, with Ray and Val Lillas in their ranch-type house smothered in climbing flowers. Val and Ray were the parents of two children, Maree, nineteen and just married, and seventeen-year-old Steve. Faced with a headlong plunge into Australian society, Hue Hue did not hesitate. Val took her to her room, white-walled and hung with pleasant landscape pictures; the floor was carpeted in beige and a window overlooked an ivy hedge and the garden beyond. It was Hue Hue's personal quarters, as had been the cabin on the white ship; only this was a room full of life, not death.

That evening they all watched the six o'clock TV news. Hue Hue had never in her life even seen TV, and there she was spotlighted and plied with questions in the middle of the screen. Her favorite actress, Chan Chan, could hardly have been the object of such adulation. Hue Hue watched entranced until Val was tempted to break the spell. Waving at the little girl on the screen, she called, "Hullo, Hue Hue!" and Hue Hue suddenly came out of her dream. To Ly To, who interpreted for Val and Ray, she said: "They all seem to take me for someone important. Well, maybe they're right!" For the first time she felt a little proud of herself.

21

In rather less comfortable quarters on Pulau Bidong, Hue Hue's father had received a letter dated June 5, 1979, from the Malaysian Red Crescent confirming that Hue Hue was in Australia: "Address unknown. But she knows of your presence in Malaysia and will contact you soon."

The day before, Hue Hue, just beginning to come to her senses in her new surroundings, sat down and wrote to her father. She outlined all that had happened since that fateful night in September nine months ago, when they had been separated; told him of Ladd Reef and her rescue by the Mangsee fishermen of Palawan and of her new home in Australia. She begged him to come quickly to join her with the family.

The letter reached Tinh in mid-June. Confronted by this tangible proof of Hue Hue's existence, both Le Mai and Tinh cheered up. Tinh had been harboring dark thoughts about his daughter's sanity. After all her sufferings, could she still be normal, he wondered, or had she been degraded into some kind of half-savage monster? The clear, bold characters of Hue Hue's letter put all doubt from his mind. His sole aim now was to join her in Australia.

Since her arrival at Pulau Bidong, Le Mai had been in poor health. She was too ill to travel until in August the office of the UN High Commissioner for Refugees in Kuala Lumpur arranged for her and the family to be ferried to the mainland. They made the twenty-mile crossing to Trengganu on August 13. Tinh and the boys were then installed at the UN transit camp, Belfield, at Kuala Lumpur. Le Mai was taken to a hospital. She needed time and peace—impossible to find in a refugee camp—to recover her health and get accustomed to her sorrows: the loss of her son Trung, of her sister Binh, of her cousin Dan. She sadly missed her mother and father in Vietnam. With a baby due in three months, she felt unsure of the future, unable to believe that she and her family would ever be reunited with Hue Hue.

For Hue Hue, meanwhile, the crucial question was not if her family would come, but when. As far as the Australian immigration people could say, it would be the end of August. The news reassured Hue Hue, who, with her accustomed energy, threw herself into the process of becoming Australian. By mid-June the school formalities were fixed, and she started off to school. Until the end of the month, Val drove her to the school at Beverly Hills, twenty minutes away, for an intensive course of English and allied subjects. Then, after a few trips with Val by train, Hue Hue was on her own. She spent her days at school being weaned from her Chinese-Vietnamese ways to the life of Australia, and learning the English language. Soon she was talking of her father and mother as Mum and Dad. For herself she chose a new name, Karen. Everywhere Val went, Hue Hue went too—shopping, tea parties, even a wedding or two; she was "integrating" naturally, intelligently, and rapidly becoming Australianized. She was in no hurry, on the other hand, to lose her hand or her taste for her native cuisine. She and Val took turns cooking the dinner, one evening Australian style, the next Cantonese or Vietnamese. Hue Hue's reputation as a cook spread, and as more people came to the house to taste her oriental dishes, the more her circle of friends widened.

But Hue Hue was troubled. The end of August came, but with it no sign of her parents. Ly To telephoned saying that they were now expected on October 15, but a few days before the fifteenth he called again to explain that the family's departure from Malaysia was once more delayed; Le Mai was still in the hospital. At that news Hue Hue, always so self-possessed, burst into tears and ran to her room. For the next few days she hardly spoke. Outside school, she seemed to have lost interest in everything, even cooking.

A week later, just after Hue Hue had left for school, the telephone rang in Val's home. It was Mr. Robson of the Immigration Department. "Well, this time I have some good news for you," he told Val. "The family's arrival in Sydney is confirmed for October twenty-fifth." Val wrote out the message and gave it to Hue Hue when she returned from school. Hue Hue read it, then looked at Val. "I can't believe it," she said, then threw her arms around Val's neck and hugged her.

Early in the afternoon of October 25, after flying from Kuala Lumpur, Tinh and his family reached their new home in the East Hills government hostel while Hue Hue was still at school. "Bellingen 2," a simply furnished but comfortable ground-floor apartment at the hostel, had been allotted to them. They settled in and, leaving the front door open, waited impatiently for Hue Hue. Le Mai, tired out after the flight, lay down to rest, her heart racing at the thought of seeing her daughter again.

With her school books under one arm, Hue Hue stepped off the train at East Hills station and walked through the little town and over the footbridge lying across the broad creek, then along the tarmac road leading to the hostel. As she walked on in the warm October sun past clumps of blue gum trees, her pace was more hurried than usual but her mind was calm. For more than a year, she had ceaselessly prayed for the moment that was about to happen.

At the hostel a little boy, a friend of her young brother's back in Cantho, stopped her. "They're all waiting for you," he said, and led her along the concrete-paved pathway until they were in front of of the window of Bellingen 2, where he called out, "Hue Hue's here!" In an instant Quang and To were through the open door. Momentarily they stopped short, so overcome at the sight of their sister that they could only smile incredulously at her. Then Tinh was at her side; as she flung her free arm around her father's neck both were crying. Tinh led Hue Hue inside to her mother; she hugged Le Mai, then Quang and To, in a confusion of tears and fond talk. Nothing mattered now that they were all together again. All except their beloved Trung. They asked about him, and Hue Hue told them quietly, in a few words; she could sense that, for all their joy at her return, their grief for Trung, like hers, remained inconsolable.

Tran Hue Hue

EPILOGUE

Le Mai had often been present during my talks with Hue Hue, but as they drew to an end I saw less of her on account of her visits to the hospital for checkups and a false alarm or two. Tinh and the children were all wondering, would it be a boy or girl? None of them really cared; all they knew was that by some miracle there would soon be one more of them to take the place of Trung.

On November 16, Le Mai had her baby. When I went around the next morning to see her in the Crown Street Women's Hospital in Sydney, Tinh, Hue Hue, and the boys were all there in the waiting room, with beaming smiles. "It's a boy," said Hue Hue. "We're calling him Jason. Come and see him," and she led me into her mother's ward. Le Mai was sitting up in bed. Smiling as always, rather shyly she showed me, in a cot next to her bed, her youngest son, a very beautiful-looking baby. I bent down and kissed his forehead, then expressed my warmest wishes and congratulations to his mother and father. Le Mai answered me with a few words, which Hue Hue translated. "He looks just like Trung," she said.